The Encyclopedia of
GUITARTAB
CHORDS

The unique *GuitarTab* format makes it easy to learn new chords at a glance—
it's as easy as reading tablature.

Compiled and edited by Mark Bridges and Joe Dineen

D0783313

Amsco Publications
New York/London/Sydney

Project editor: Ed Lozano
Compiled by Mark Bridges
Edited by Joe Dineen
Layout by Mark Bridges and ConceptuaLine

Order No. AM 948772
US International Standard Book Number: 0.8256.1690.5
UK International Standard Book Number: 0.7119.7596.5

Exclusive Distributors:
Music Sales Corporation
257 Park Avenue South, New York, NY 10010 USA
Music Sales Limited
8/9 Frith Street, London W1V 5TZ England
Music Sales Pty. Limited
120 Rothschild Street, Rosebery, Sydney, NSW 2018, Australia

Printed in the United States of America by
Vicks Lithograph and Printing Corporation

Contents

Introduction   5
How to Use this Book   6
Chords   7

    C   major 7
              minor 13
              dominant 17
              diminished 23
              augmented-suspended 25

    C♯/D♭ major 26
              minor 32
              dominant 36
              diminished 42
              augmented-suspended 44

    D   major 45
              minor 51
              dominant 55
              diminished 61
              augmented-suspended 63

    E♭/D♯ major 64
              minor 70
              dominant 74
              diminished 80
              augmented-suspended 82

    E   major 83
              minor 89
              dominant 93
              diminished 99
              augmented-suspended 101

    F   major 102
              minor 108
              dominant 112
              diminished 118
              augmented-suspended 120

    F♯/G♭ major 121
              minor 127
              dominant 131
              diminished 137
              augmented-suspended 139

    G   major 140
              minor 146
              dominant 150
              diminished 156
              augmented-suspended 158

Contents

Ab/G#	major	.159
	minor	.165
	dominant	.169
	diminished	.175
	augmented-suspended	.177
A	major	.178
	minor	.184
	dominant	.188
	diminished	.194
	augmented-suspended	.196
Bb/A#	major	.197
	minor	.203
	dominant	.207
	diminished	.213
	augmented-suspended	.215
B	major	.216
	minor	.222
	dominant	.226
	diminished	.232
	augmented-suspended	.234

Powerchords 235

   five .... .235

   suspended 4 .... .241

   five diminished .... .247

   major third(no5) .... .253

   major sixth(no3&5) .... .259

Slash Chords 265

Transposing 269

Introduction

This book is a reference guide for guitarists. It is not intended as a method book, but rather as a reference book of chords that are easily accessible to the beginner or advanced guitarist. Regardless of your musical interest, this book contains the majority of chords you will encounter in most styles of music (rock, jazz, country, or blues). Strong chord knowledge will help build familiarity with the fretboard and help develop flexibility in solo, accompaniment or ensemble playing.

The forty-two chord types covered in this book are:

- major
- 6
- $\frac{6}{9}$
- maj7
- maj13
- maj9
- maj9$\sharp$11
- maj7+
- maj7$\flat$5
- maj13(no9)
- add9
- minor
- m7
- m6
- m(maj7)
- m add9
- m9
- m(maj9)
- m$\frac{6}{9}$
- m11(no9)
- m11

- 7
- 9
- 13
- 7$\flat$9
- 7$\sharp$9
- 13$\flat$9
- 7+
- 7$\flat$5
- 7$^{\flat9}_{\sharp5}$
- 7$^{\sharp9}_{\sharp5}$
- 9$\sharp$11
- 9+
- 7sus4
- 9sus4
- 13sus4
- o
- m7$\flat$5
- o7
- +
- sus4
- sus2

In addition to these chord types, this book also contains special sections on Powerchords and Slash Chords further adding to the completeness of this collection. Although there are many more chord types available, these chord types were chosen for their popularity as well as their usefulness.

The Encyclopedia of GuitarTab Chords has been designed with the player in mind. You don't have to go to your bookshelf to find that bulky chord encyclopedia that your music stand can't even hold up, you don't have to break the spine of the book to get it to stay open, and it doesn't take up all the space on your music stand. It is easy-to-carry and easy-to-use. We hope that this book will serve as a valuable reference source during your years as a developing guitarist.

How to Use this Book

It is strongly recommended that you develop a practice regimen in which you devote some time to chord study. If you practice one hour each session, then devote fifteen or twenty minutes to chord study. Another approach would be to practice your warm-up exercises with a different chord type each day.

Here are some helpful tips:

• Above each chord grid you will find the name of the chord and to the right you'll find the chord spelled out on the treble staff.
• Each chord type has several variations that extend the length of the fretboard. Each variation is presented from the lowest position on the neck to the highest position on the neck.
• Use the following legend to construct the desired chord.

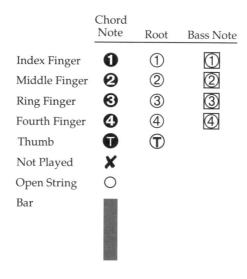

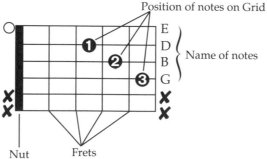

Whether you are looking to develop *chops* (technique) or broaden your chord vocabulary, *The Encyclopedia of GuitarTab Chords* is for you.

C

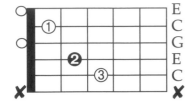

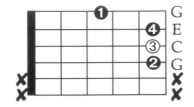

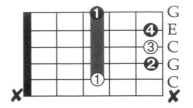

5. Fret
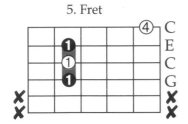

10. Fret
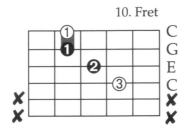

8. Fret
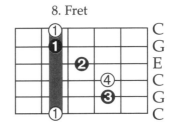

10. Fret
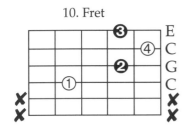

14. Fret
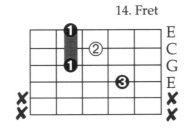

8. Fret
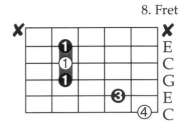

12. Fret
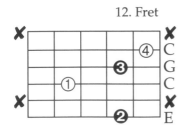

C

C6

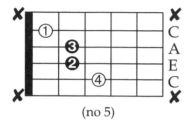   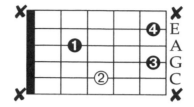   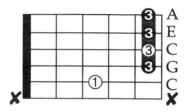

(no 5)

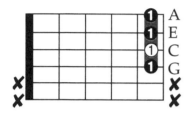   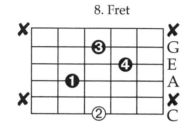   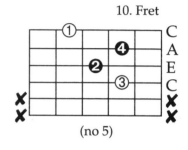

8. Fret   10. Fret

(no 5)

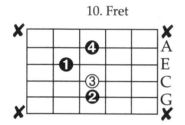   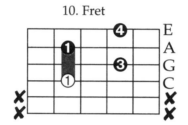

10. Fret   10. Fret

C 6/9

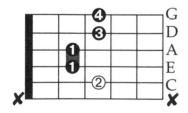   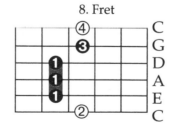   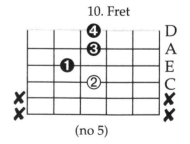

8. Fret   10. Fret

(no 5)

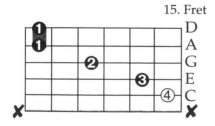

15. Fret

C

Cmaj7

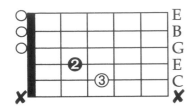

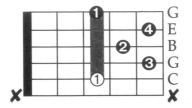

5. Fret

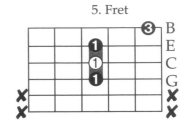

10. Fret

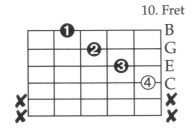

8. Fret

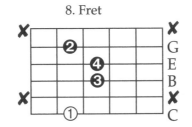

8. Fret

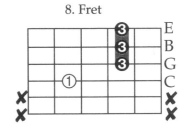

15. Fret

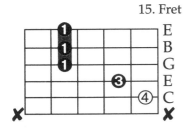

Cmaj13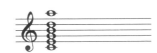

8. Fret

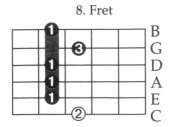

8. Fret

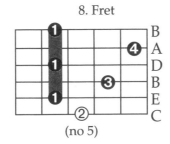

(no 5)

8. Fret

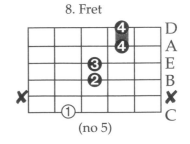

(no 5)

C

Cmaj9

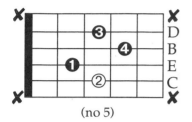

(no 5)

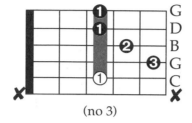

(no 3)

8. Fret

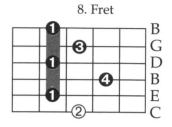

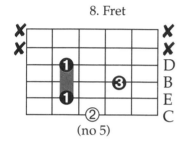

(no 5)

8. Fret

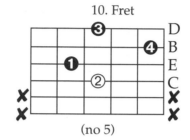

(no 5)

10. Fret

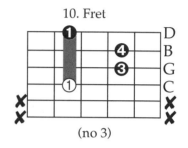

(no 3)

10. Fret

Cmaj9#11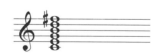

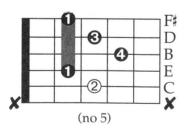

(no 5)

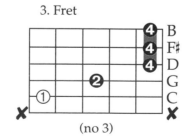

3. Fret

(no 3)

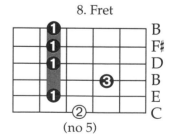

8. Fret

(no 5)

C

Cmaj7+

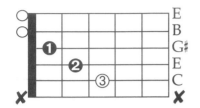

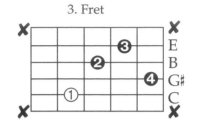

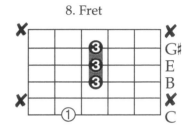

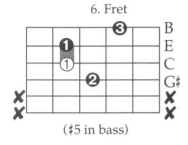

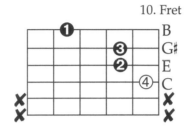

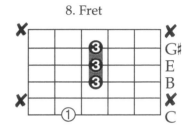

(♯5 in bass)

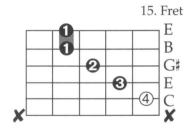

Cmaj7♭5

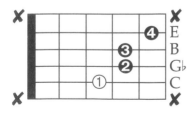

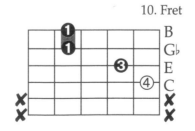

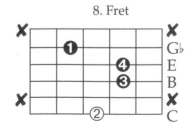

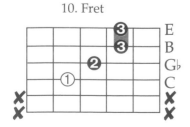

C

Cmaj13(no9)

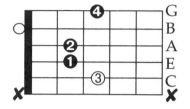 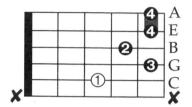 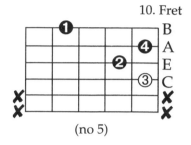

(no 5)

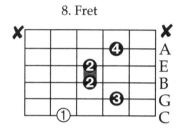

8. Fret

Cadd9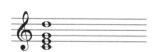

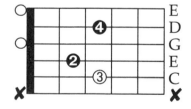 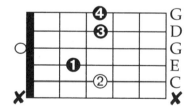 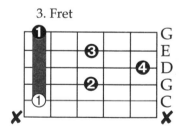

3. Fret

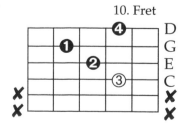 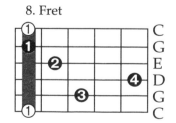

10. Fret   8. Fret

Cm

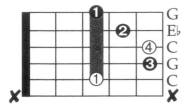

10. Fret

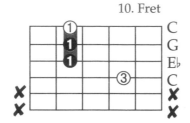

8. Fret

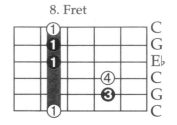

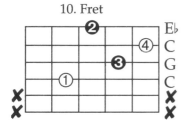

10. Fret

13. Fret

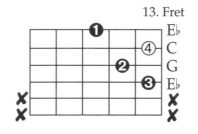

6. Fret

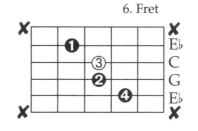

Cm7

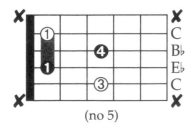

(no 5)

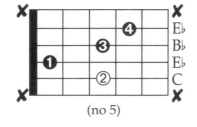

(no 5)

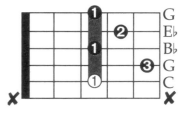

8. Fret

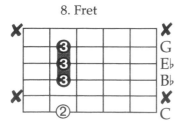

8. Fret

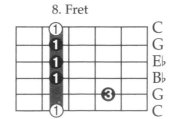

10. Fret

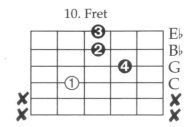

C

Cm6

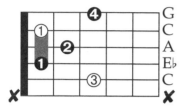
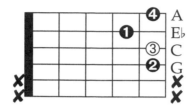
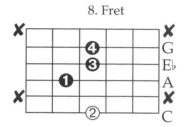

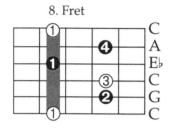
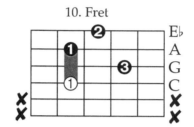

Cm(maj7)

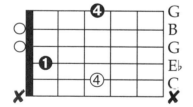
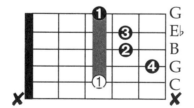
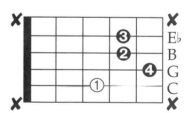

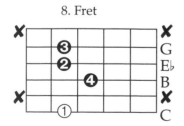
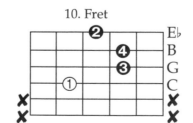
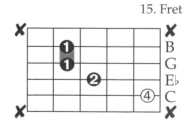

Cm add9

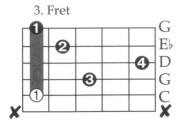

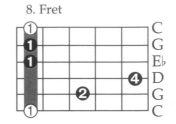

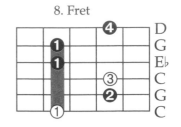

Cm9

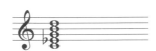

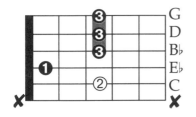

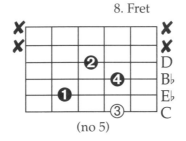

(no 5)

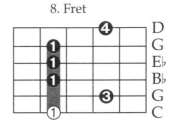

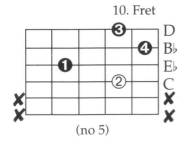

(no 5)

Cm(maj9)

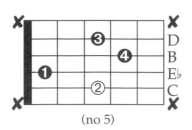

(no 5)

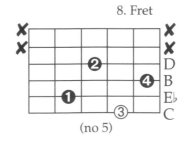

(no 5)

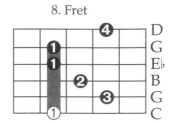

C

Cm⁶₉

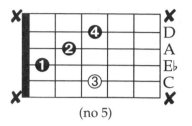

(no 5)

8. Fret

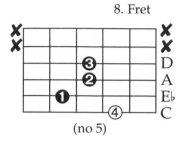

(no 5)

10. Fret

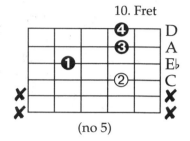

(no 5)

8. Fret

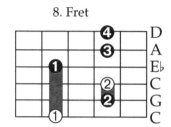

Cm11(no9)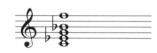

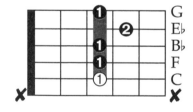

10. Fret

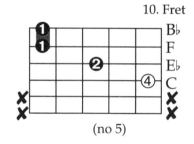

(no 5)

8. Fret

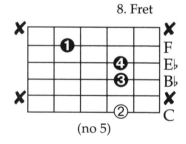

(no 5)

Cm11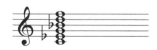

8. Fret

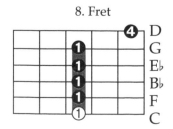

C7

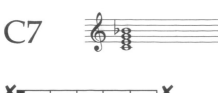

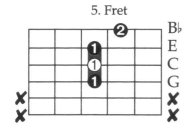

(no 5)

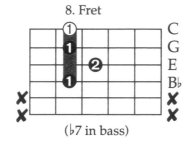

3. Fret

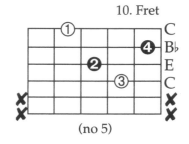

5. Fret

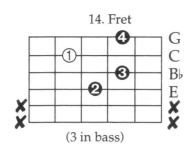

8. Fret

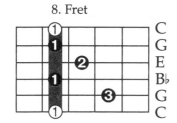

(♭7 in bass)

10. Fret

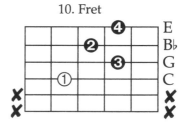

(no 5)

8. Fret

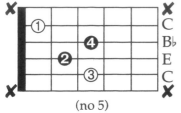

8. Fret

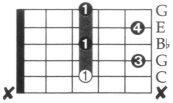

10. Fret

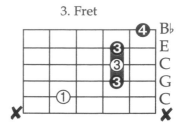

14. Fret

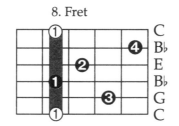

(3 in bass)

C

C9

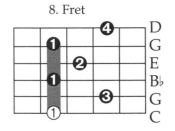

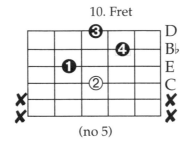

(no 5)

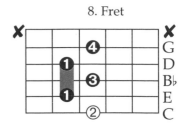

8. Fret

8. Fret

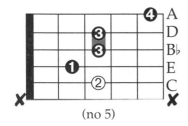

8. Fret

10. Fret

(no 5)

C13

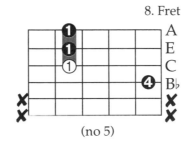

8. Fret

8. Fret

(no 5)

(no 5)

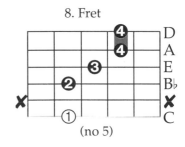

8. Fret

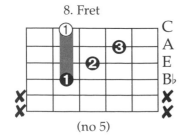

8. Fret

(no 5)

(no 5)

C7♭9

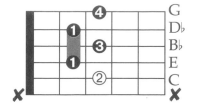

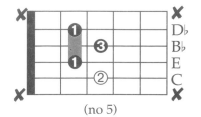

(no 5)

G D♭ B♭ E C

8. Fret

(no 5)

10. Fret

(no 5)

C7♯9

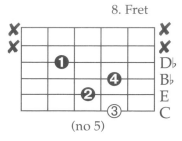

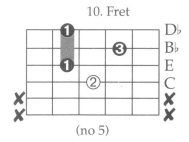

(no 5)

8. Fret

8. Fret

10. Fret

(no 5)

C13♭9

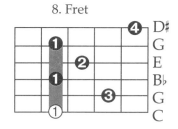

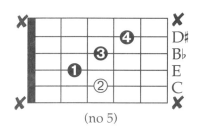

(no 5)

8. Fret

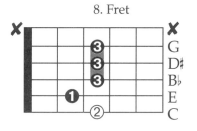

(no 5)

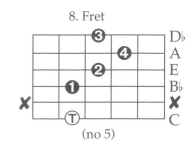

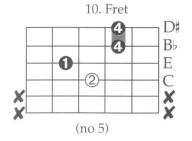

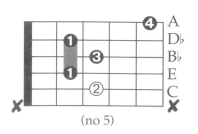

C

C7+

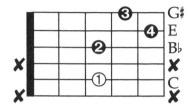

3. Fret

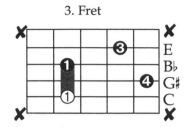

8. Fret

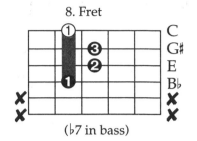

(♭7 in bass)

8. Fret

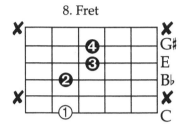

10. Fret

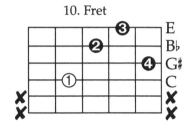

C7♭5

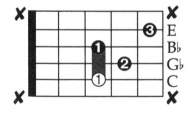

4. Fret

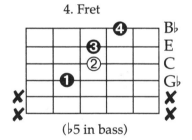

(♭5 in bass)

8. Fret

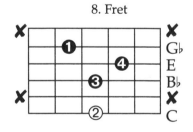

8. Fret

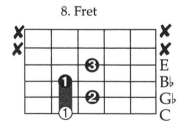

10. Fret

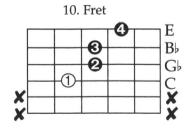

C7$^{\flat 9}_{\sharp 5}$

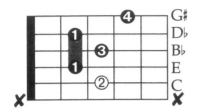

8. Fret

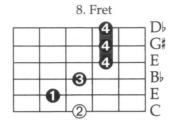

C7$^{\sharp 9}_{\sharp 5}$

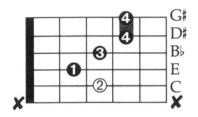

8. Fret

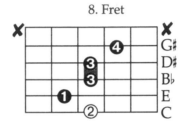

C9$\sharp$11

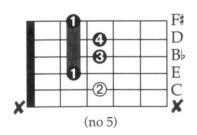

(no 5)

8. Fret

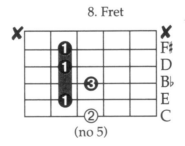

(no 5)

C9+

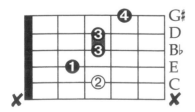

8. Fret

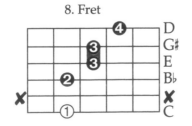

C

C7sus4

(no 5)

3. Fret
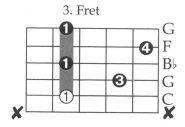
G
F
B♭
G
C

5. Fret
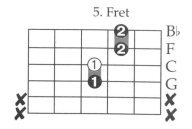
B♭
F
C
G

8. Fret
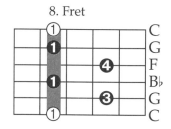
C
G
F
B♭
G
C

10. Fret
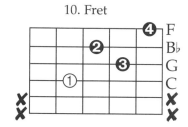
F
B♭
G
C

C9sus4

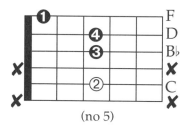
F
D
B♭
C
(no 5)

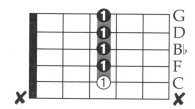
G
D
B♭
F
C

8. Fret
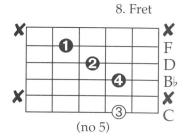
F
D
B♭
C
(no 5)

10. Fret
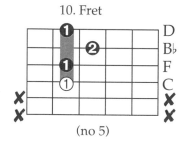
D
B♭
F
C
(no 5)

C13sus4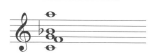

3. Fret
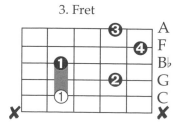
A
F
B♭
G
C

8. Fret
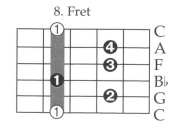
C
A
F
B♭
G
C

C°

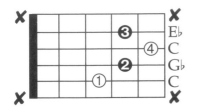

8. Fret

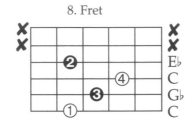

13. Fret

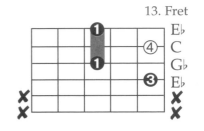

Cm7♭5

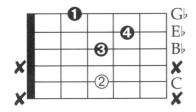

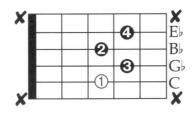

8. Fret

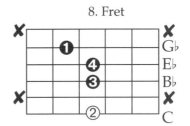

8. Fret

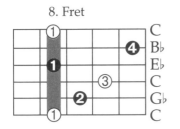

10. Fret

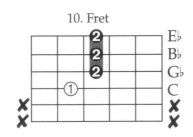

C

$C°7$

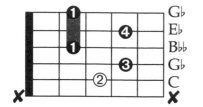   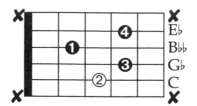   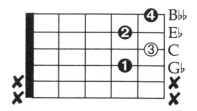

7. Fret   8. Fret   8. Fret

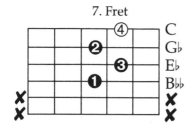   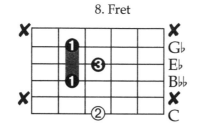   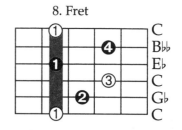

10. Fret

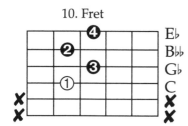

C

C+

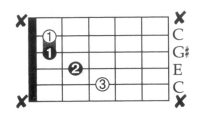

8. Fret

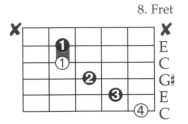

10. Fret

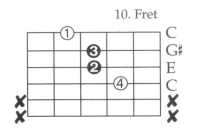

Csus4

3. Fret

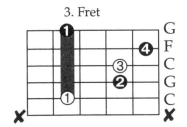

5. Fret

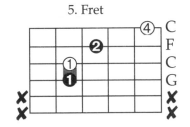

8. Fret

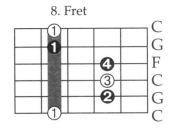

10. Fret

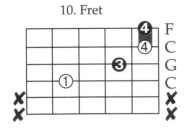

Csus2

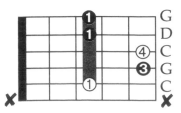

8. Fret

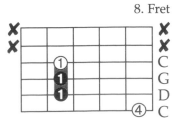

10. Fret

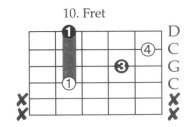

C#

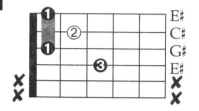

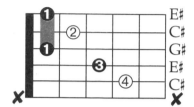

6. Fret
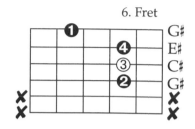

4. Fret
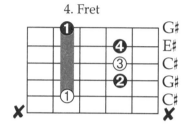

6. Fret
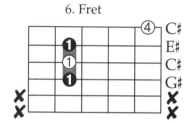

11. Fret
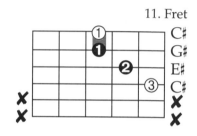

9. Fret
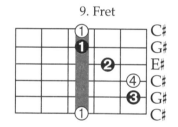

11. Fret
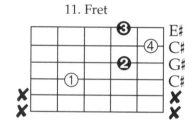

9. Fret
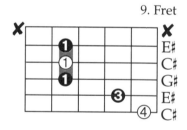

13. Fret
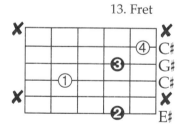

C#6

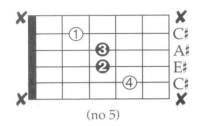

(no 5)

4. Fret

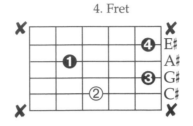

4. Fret

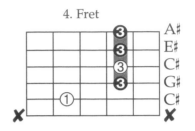

6. Fret

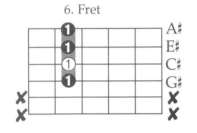

9. Fret

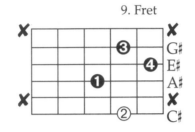

11. Fret

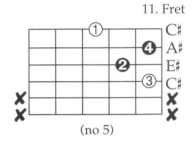

(no 5)

11. Fret

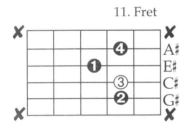

11. Fret

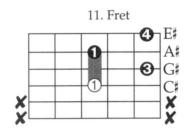

C#⁶₉

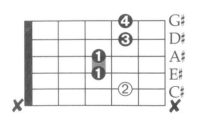

9. Fret

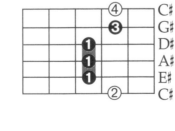

11. Fret

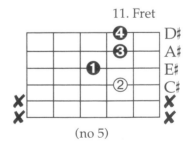

(no 5)

16. Fret

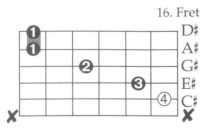

C#maj7

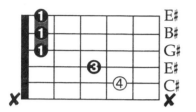

	4. Fret	6. Fret
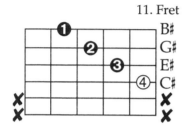	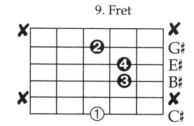	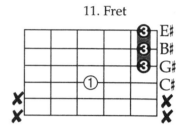

11. Fret	9. Fret	11. Fret
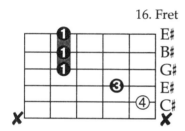	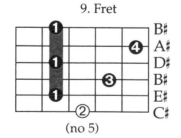	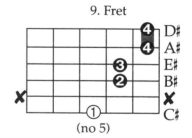

16. Fret

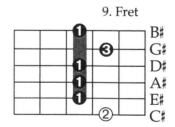

C#maj13

9. Fret	9. Fret	9. Fret
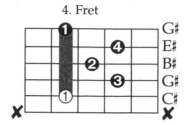	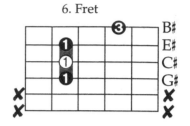	(no 5)

(no 5)   (no 5)

C#maj9

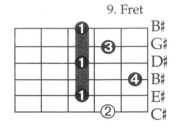

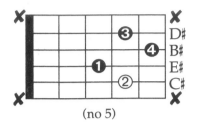
(no 5)

4. Fret
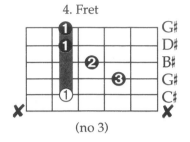
(no 3)

9. Fret
(no 5)

9. Fret
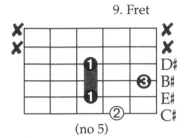
(no 5)

11. Fret
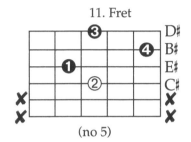
(no 5)

11. Fret
(no 3)

C#maj9#11

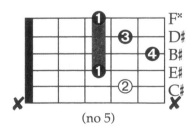
(no 5)

4. Fret
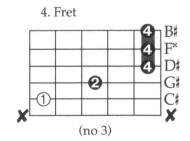
(no 3)

9. Fret
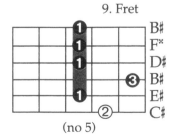
(no 5)

C♯maj7+

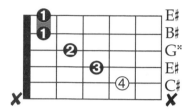

4. Fret

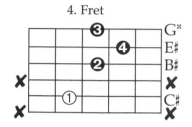

4. Fret

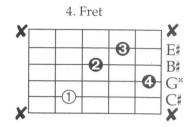

7. Fret

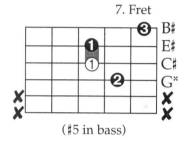

(♯5 in bass)

11. Fret

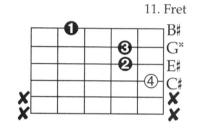

9. Fret

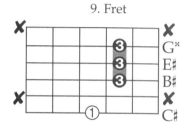

16. Fret

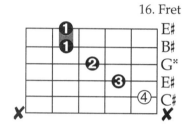

C♯maj7♭5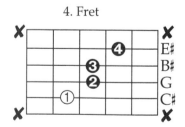

4. Fret

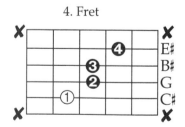

11. Fret

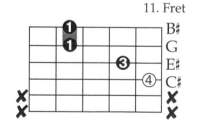

9. Fret

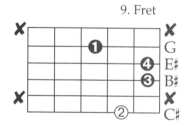

11. Fret

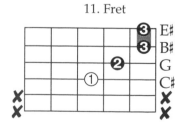

C#maj13(no9)

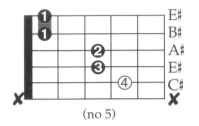
(no 5)

4. Fret

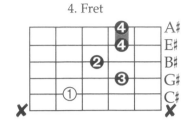

11. Fret

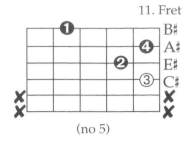
(no 5)

9. Fret

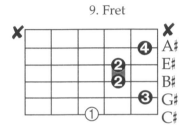

C#add9

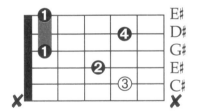

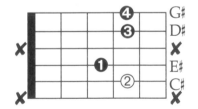

4. Fret

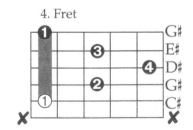

11. Fret

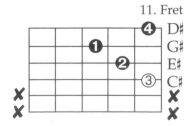

9. Fret

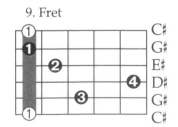

C♯m

4. Fret
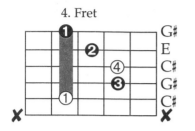

11. Fret
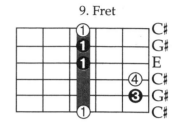

9. Fret
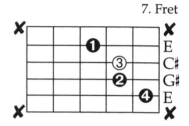

11. Fret
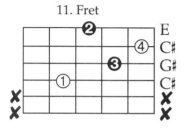

14. Fret
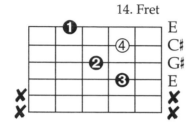

7. Fret
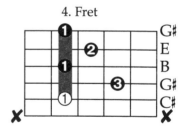

C♯m7

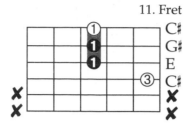

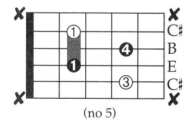

(no 5)

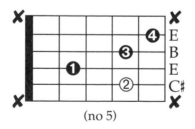

(no 5)

4. Fret

9. Fret
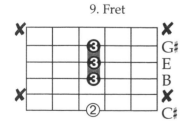

9. Fret
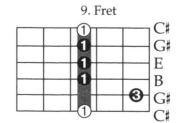

11. Fret
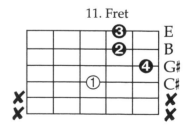

C#m6

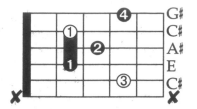

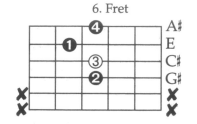

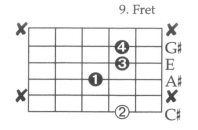

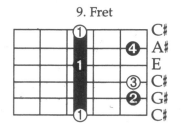

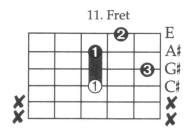

C#m(maj7)

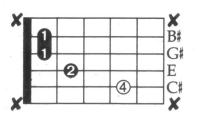

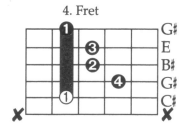

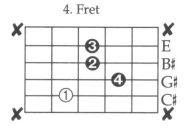

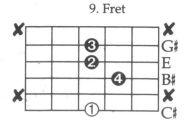

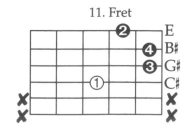

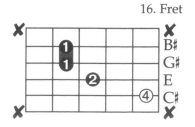

C#
Db

C♯m add9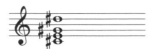

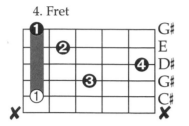
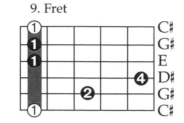
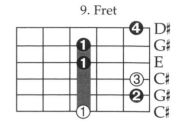

C♯m9

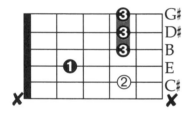
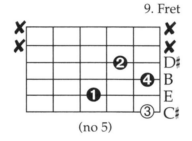
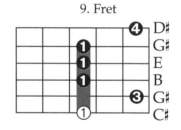

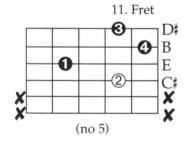

C♯m(maj9)

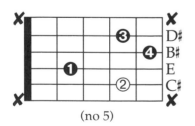
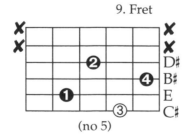
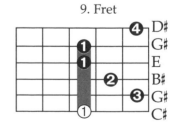

C#m$^6_9$

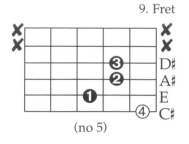

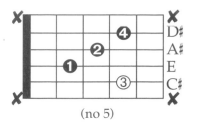

(no 5)

9. Fret

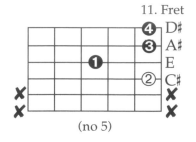

(no 5)

11. Fret

(no 5)

9. Fret

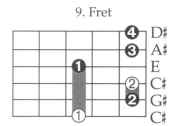

C#m11(no9)

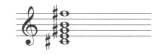

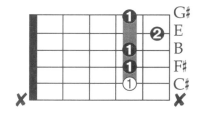

11. Fret

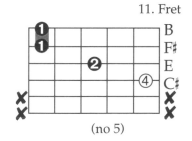

(no 5)

9. Fret

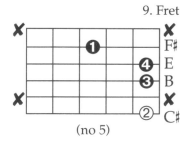

(no 5)

C#m11

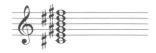

9. Fret

C♯7

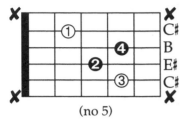

(no 5)

4. Fret

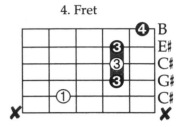

4. Fret

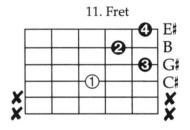

6. Fret

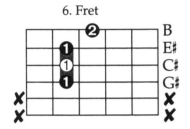

9. Fret

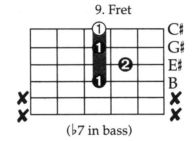

(♭7 in bass)

11. Fret

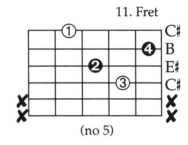

(no 5)

9. Fret

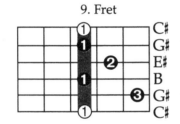

9. Fret

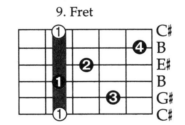

11. Fret

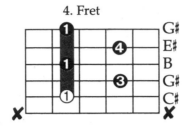

15. Fret

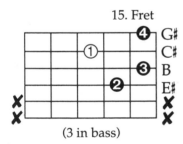

(3 in bass)

C#9

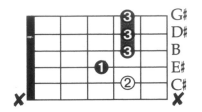

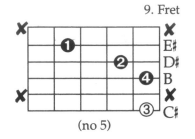

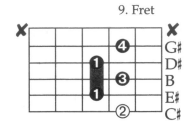

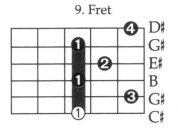

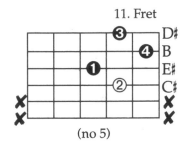

C#13

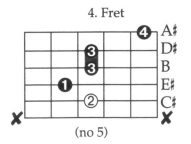

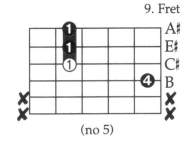

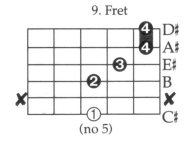

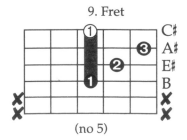

C#7♭9

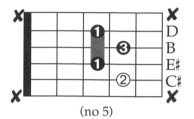

(no 5)

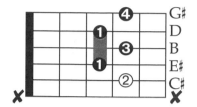

9. Fret

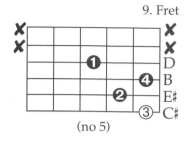

(no 5)

11. Fret

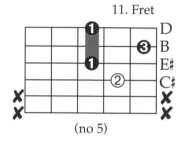

(no 5)

C#7#9

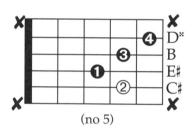

(no 5)

9. Fret

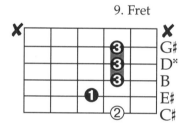

9. Fret

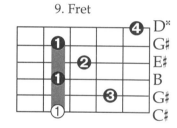

11. Fret

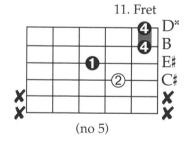

(no 5)

C#13♭9

4. Fret

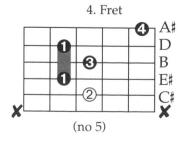

(no 5)

9. Fret

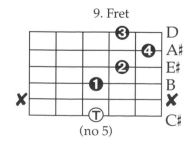

(no 5)

C#7+

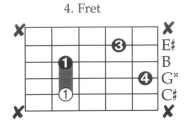

4. Fret

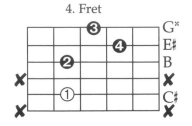

4. Fret

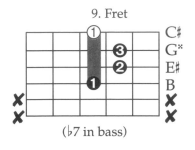

9. Fret

(♭7 in bass)

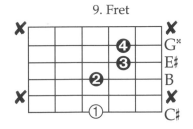

9. Fret

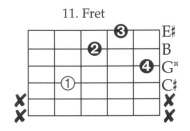

11. Fret

C#7♭5

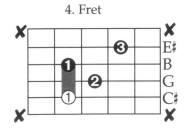

4. Fret

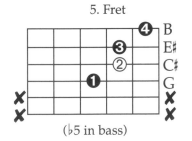

5. Fret

(♭5 in bass)

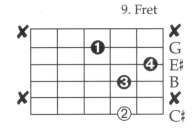

9. Fret

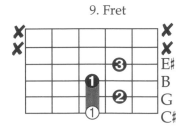

9. Fret

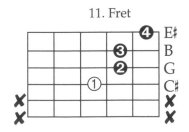

11. Fret

C♯
D♭

C♯7 ♭9 #5

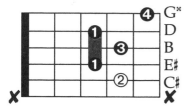

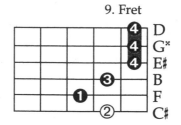

9. Fret

C♯7 #9 #5

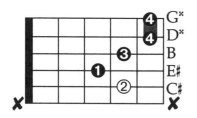

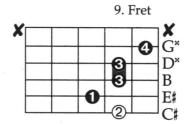

9. Fret

C♯9#11

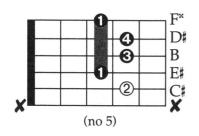

(no 5)

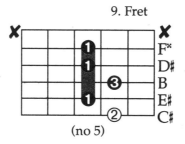

9. Fret

(no 5)

C♯9+

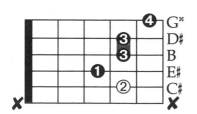

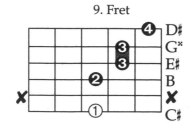

9. Fret

C#7sus4

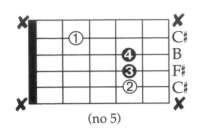

(no 5)

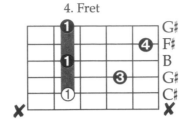

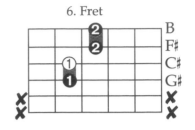

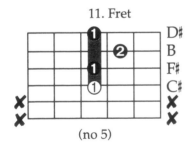

C#9sus4

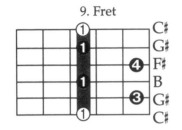

(no 5)

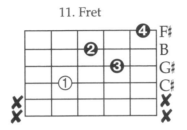

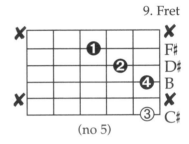

(no 5)

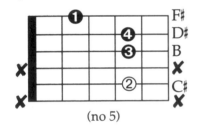

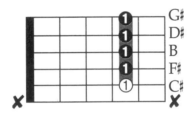

(no 5)

C#13sus4

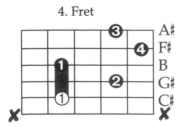

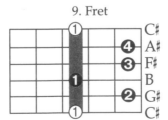

C♯ C♯°

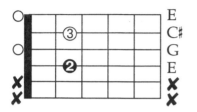

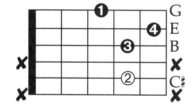

4. Fret

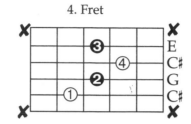

9. Fret

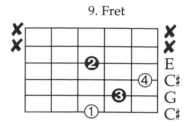

C♯m7♭5

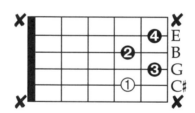

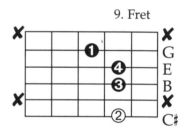

9. Fret

11. Fret

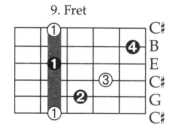

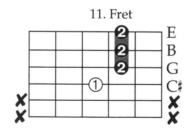

C#°7

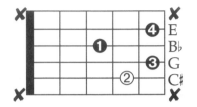

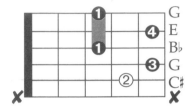

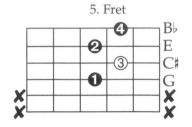

5. Fret

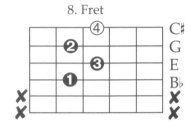

8. Fret

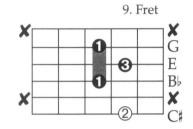

9. Fret

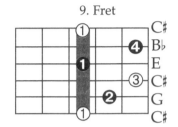

9. Fret

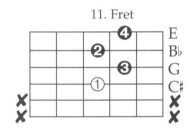

11. Fret

C♯+

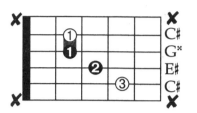 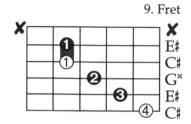 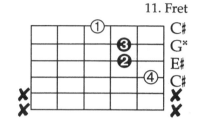

C♯sus4

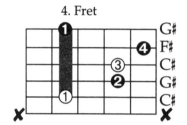 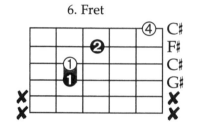 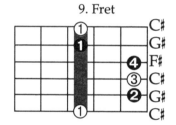

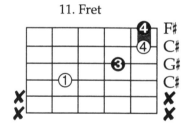

C♯sus2

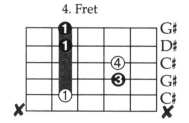 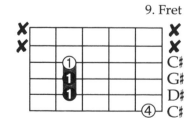 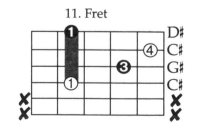

D

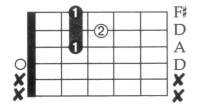
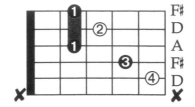

7. Fret

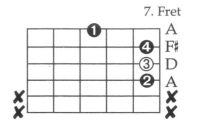

D

5. Fret

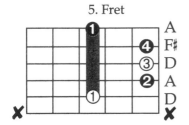

7. Fret

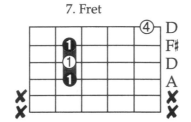

12. Fret

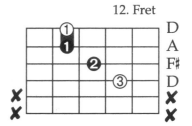

10. Fret

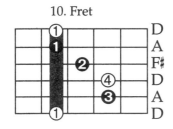

12. Fret

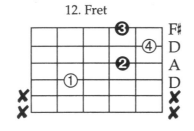

10. Fret

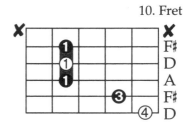

14. Fret

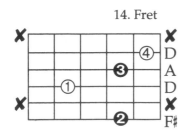

D6

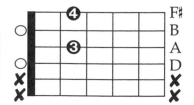

F#
B
A
D

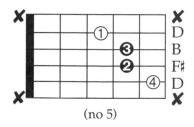

D
B
F#
D

(no 5)

5. Fret

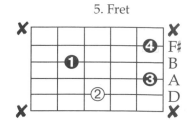

F#
B
A
D

5. Fret

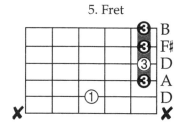

B
F#
D
A
D

7. Fret

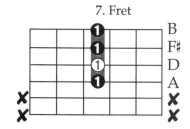

B
F#
D
A

10. Fret

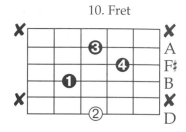

A
F#
B
D

12. Fret

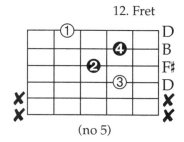

D
B
F#
D

(no 5)

12. Fret

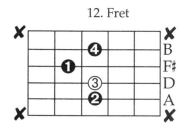

B
F#
D
A

D $\frac{6}{9}$

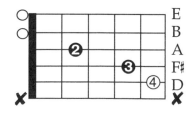

E
B
A
F#
D

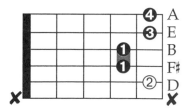

A
E
B
F#
D

10. Fret

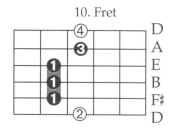

D
A
E
B
F#
D

12. Fret

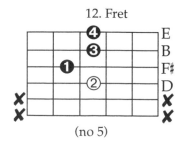

E
B
F#
D

(no 5)

Dmaj7

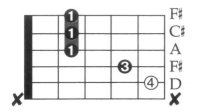

5. Fret

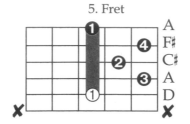

7. Fret

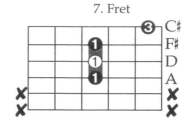

D

12. Fret

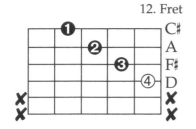

10. Fret

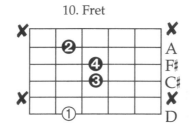

10. Fret

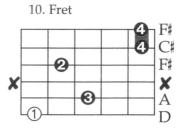

12. Fret

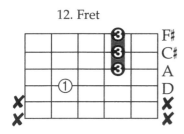

Dmaj13

10. Fret

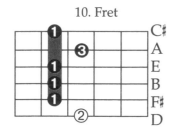

10. Fret

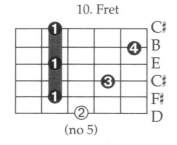

(no 5)

10. Fret

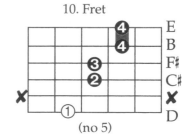

(no 5)

Dmaj9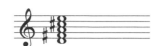

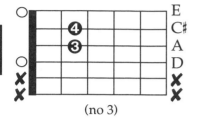

(no 3)

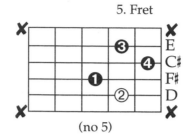

5. Fret

(no 5)

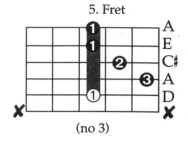

5. Fret

(no 3)

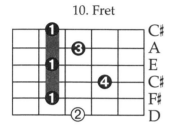

10. Fret

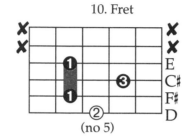

10. Fret

(no 5)

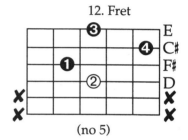

12. Fret

(no 5)

Dmaj9♯11

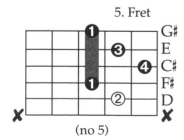

5. Fret

(no 5)

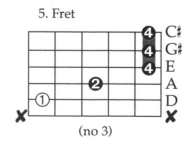

5. Fret

(no 3)

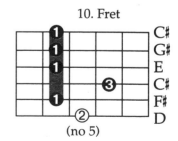

10. Fret

(no 5)

Dmaj7+

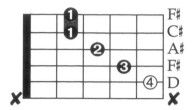

F#
C#
A#
F#
D

5. Fret

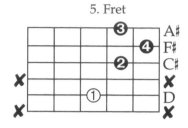

A#
F#
C#
D

5. Fret

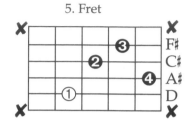

F#
C#
A#
D

D

8. Fret

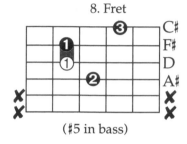

C#
F#
D
A#

(#5 in bass)

12. Fret

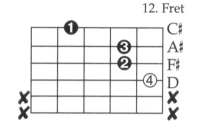

C#
A#
F#
D

10. Fret

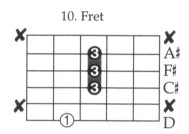

A#
F#
C#
D

Dmaj7♭5

F#
C#
A♭
D

5. Fret

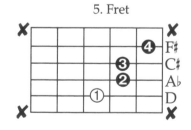

F#
C#
A♭
D

12. Fret

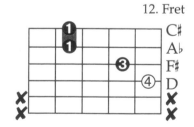

C#
A♭
F#
D

10. Fret

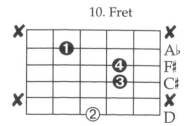

A♭
F#
C#
D

Dmaj13(no9)

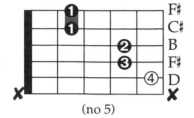

(no 5)

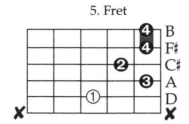

5. Fret

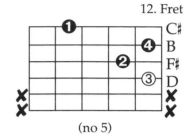

12. Fret

(no 5)

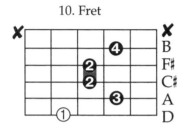

10. Fret

Dadd9

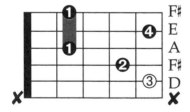

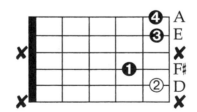

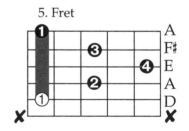

5. Fret

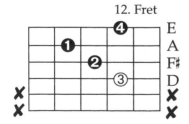

12. Fret

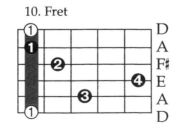

10. Fret

Dm

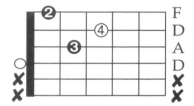

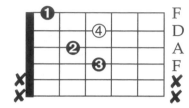

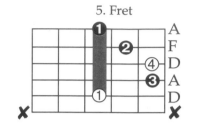

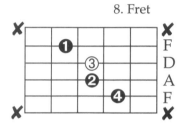

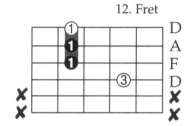

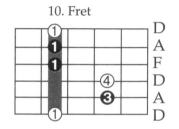

Dm7

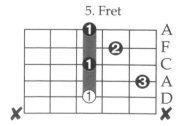

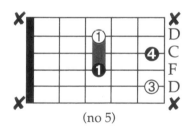

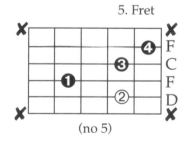

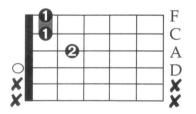

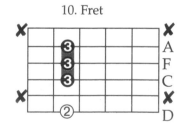

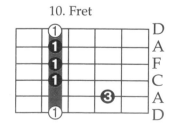

D

Dm6

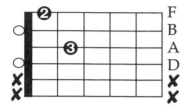

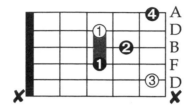

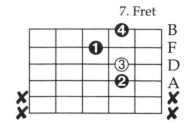

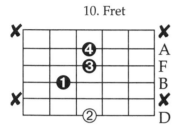

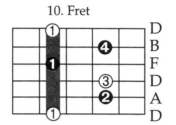

Dm(maj7)

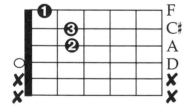

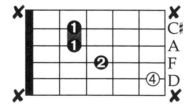

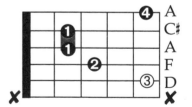

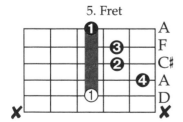

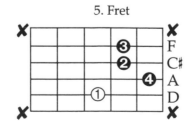

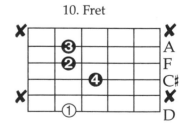

Dm add9

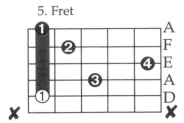 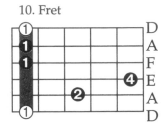 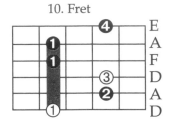

D

Dm9

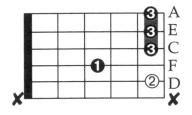 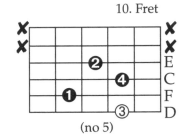 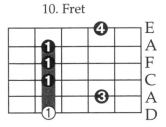

(no 5)

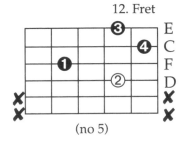

(no 5)

Dm(maj9)

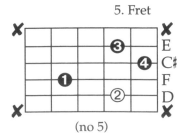 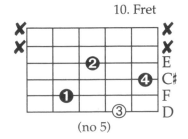 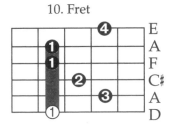

(no 5)

(no 5)

Dm$^6_9$

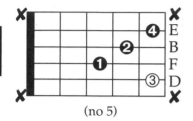

(no 5)

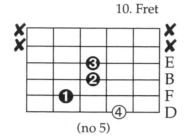

10. Fret

(no 5)

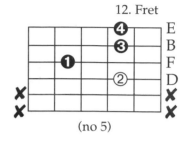

12. Fret

(no 5)

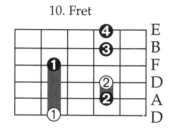

10. Fret

Dm11(no9)

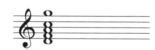

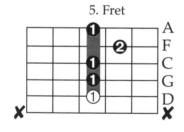

5. Fret

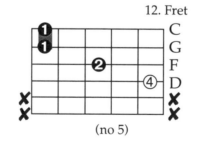

12. Fret

(no 5)

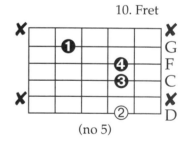

10. Fret

(no 5)

Dm11

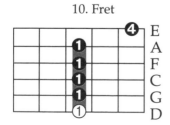

10. Fret

D7

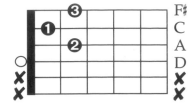

(no 5)

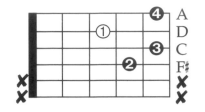

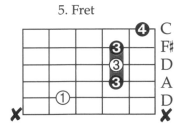

5. Fret

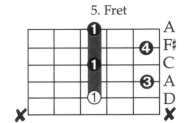

5. Fret

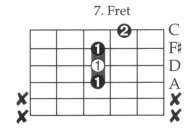

7. Fret

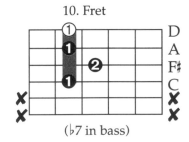

10. Fret

(♭7 in bass)

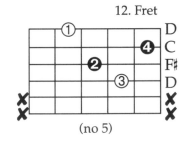

12. Fret

(no 5)

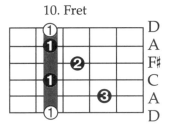

10. Fret

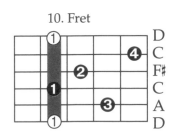

10. Fret

D9

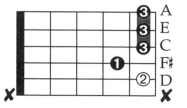
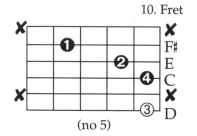
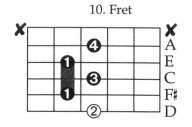

(no 5)

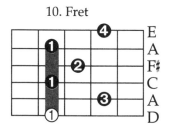
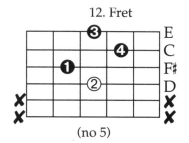

(no 5)

D13

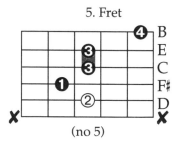
(no 5)

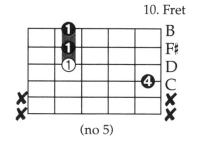
(no 5)

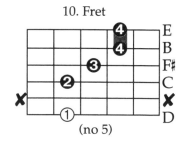
(no 5)

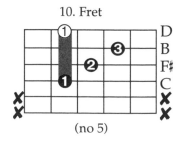
(no 5)

D7♭9

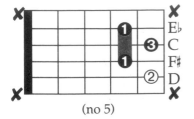

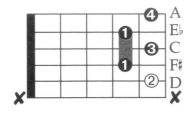

10. Fret

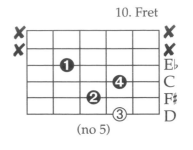

(no 5)   (no 5)   (no 5)

12. Fret

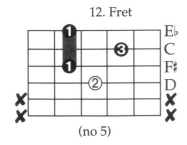

(no 5)

D7♯9

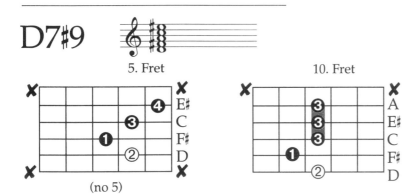

5. Fret   10. Fret   10. Fret

(no 5)

12. Fret

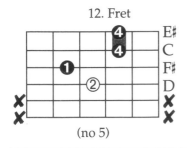

(no 5)

D13♭9

5. Fret   10. Fret

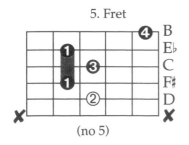   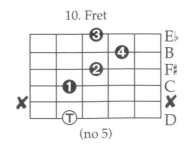

(no 5)   (no 5)

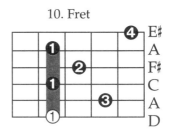

D

D7+

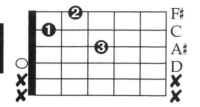

5. Fret
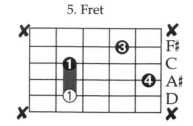

5. Fret
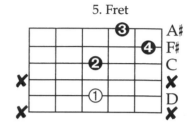

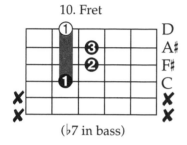

(♭7 in bass)

10. Fret
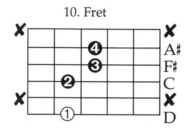

D7♭5

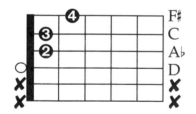

5. Fret
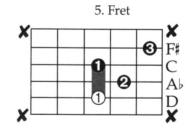

6. Fret
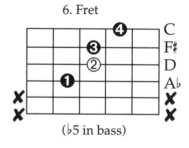

(♭5 in bass)

10. Fret
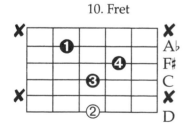

10. Fret
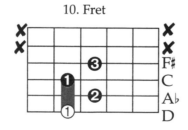

D7 ♭9 ♯5

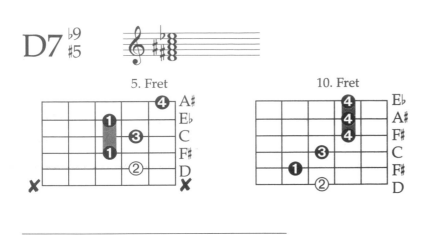

D7 ♯9 ♯5

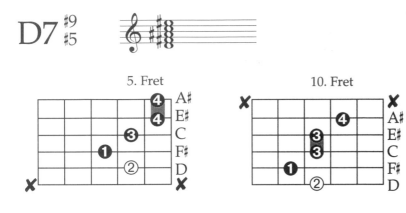

D9♯11

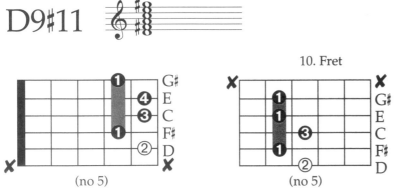

D9+

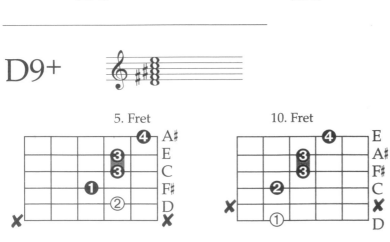

D

D7sus4

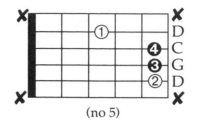

(no 5)

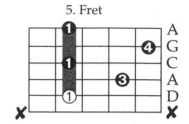

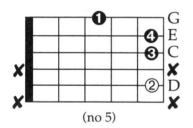

D9sus4

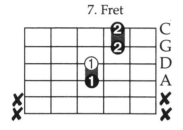

(no 5)

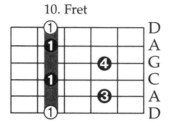

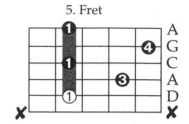

(no 5)

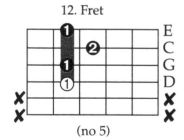

(no 5)

D13sus4

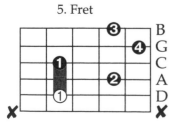

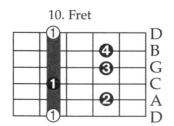

D°

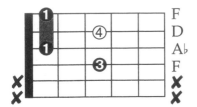

5. Fret

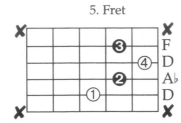

10. Fret

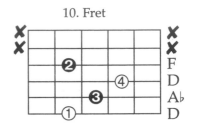

D

Dm7♭5

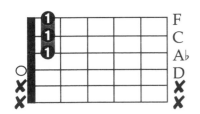

5. Fret

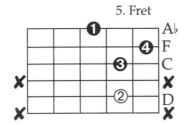

5. Fret

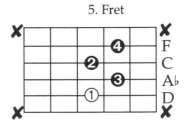

10. Fret

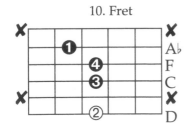

10. Fret

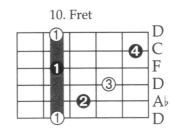

D°7

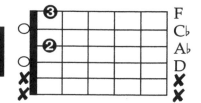

F
Cb
Ab
D
✗
✗

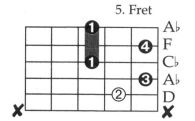

5. Fret

Ab
F
Cb
Ab
D
✗

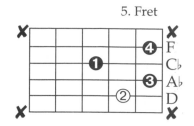

5. Fret

F
Cb
Ab
D

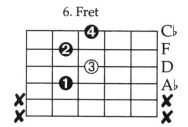

6. Fret

Cb
F
D
Ab
✗
✗

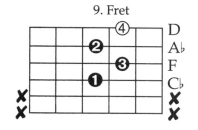

9. Fret

D
Ab
F
Cb
✗
✗

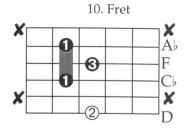

10. Fret

Ab
F
Cb
D

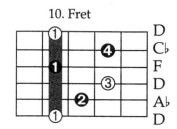

10. Fret

D
Cb
F
D
Ab
D

D+

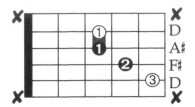

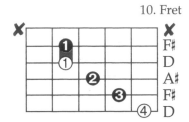

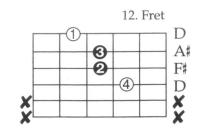

D

Dsus4

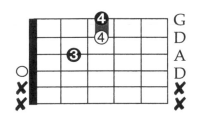

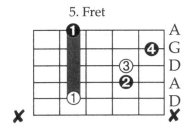

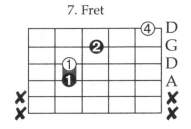

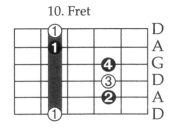

Dsus2

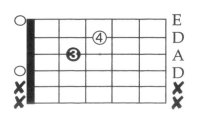

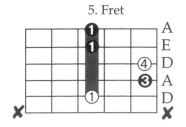

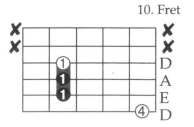

E♭

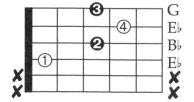 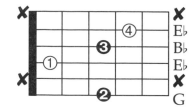 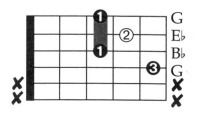

6. Fret   8. Fret   6. Fret

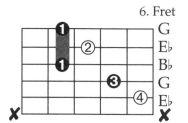 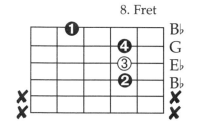 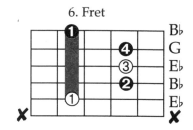

8. Fret   13. Fret   11. Fret

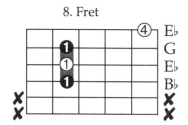 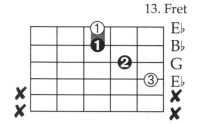 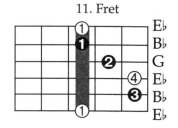

11. Fret

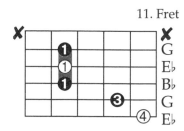

E♭6

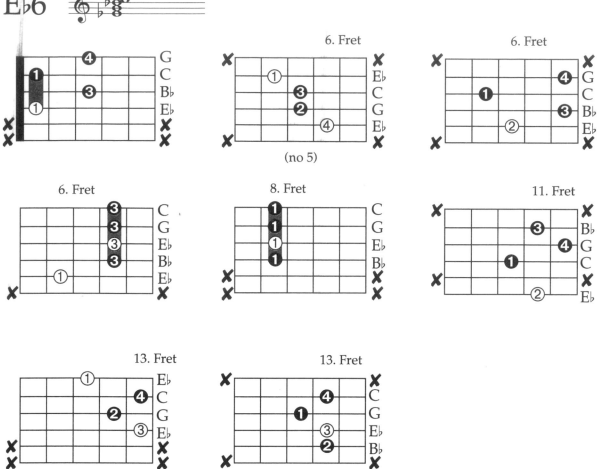

E♭$\frac{6}{9}$

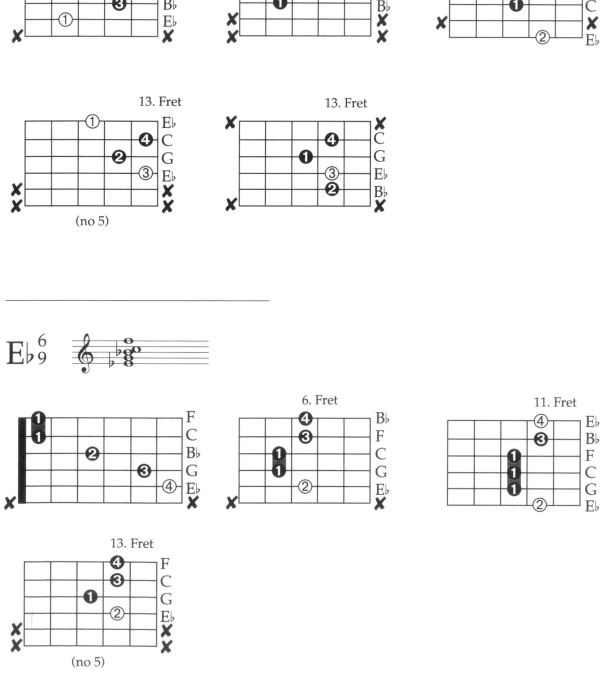

E♭maj7

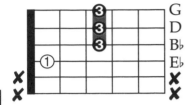

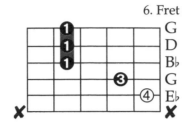

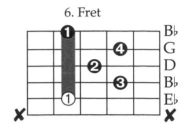

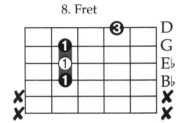

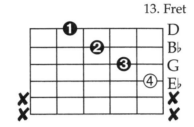

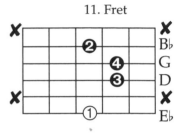

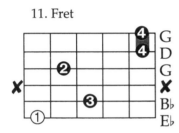

E♭maj13

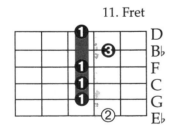

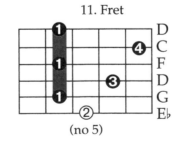

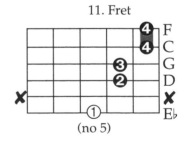

E♭maj9

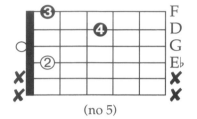
(no 5)

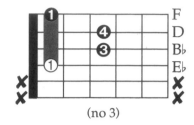
(no 3)

6. Fret
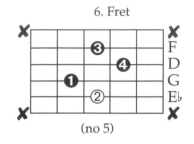
(no 5)

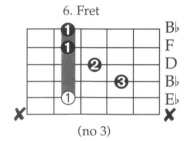
(no 3)

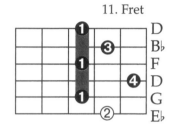

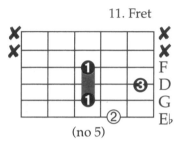
(no 5)

E♭ / D♯

E♭maj9♯11

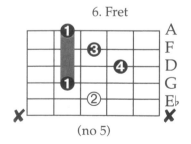
(no 5)

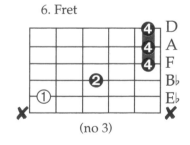
(no 3)

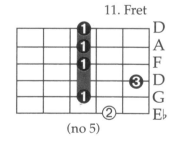
(no 5)

E♭maj7+

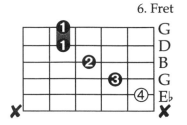

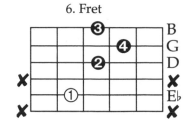

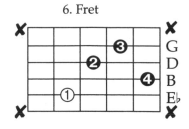

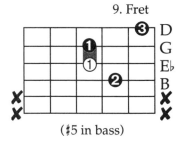

(♯5 in bass)

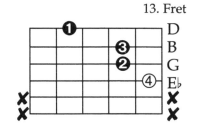

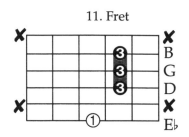

E♭maj7♭5

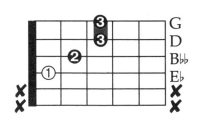

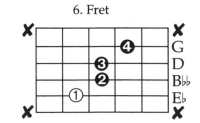

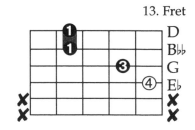

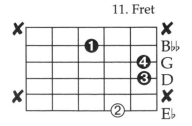

E♭maj13(no9)

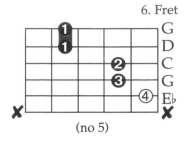

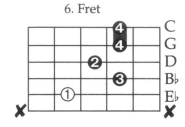

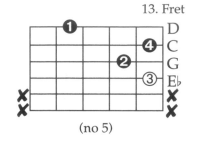

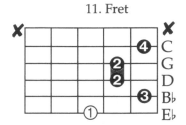

E♭add9

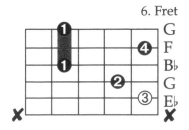

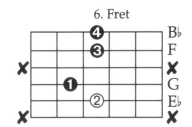

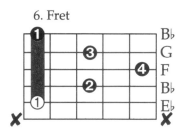

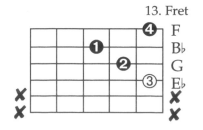

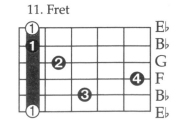

Ebm

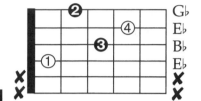

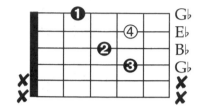

6. Fret
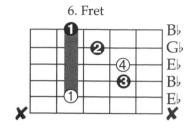

13. Fret
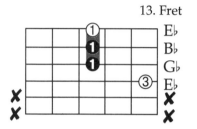

11. Fret
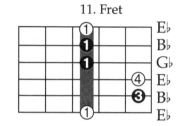

9. Fret
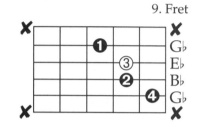

Ebm7

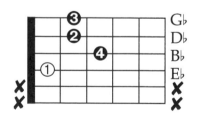

6. Fret
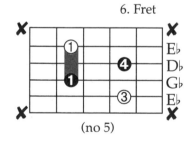

(no 5)

6. Fret
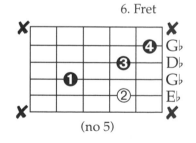

(no 5)

6. Fret
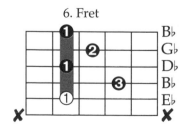

11. Fret
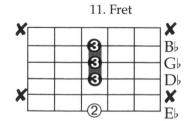

11. Fret
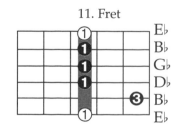

E♭m6

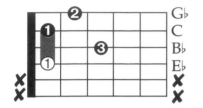

6. Fret

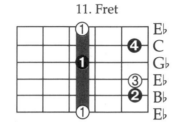

8. Fret

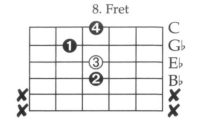

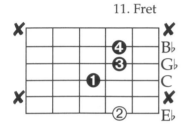

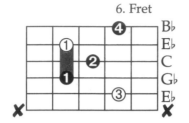

E♭m(maj7)

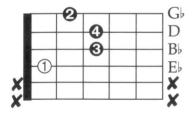

6. Fret

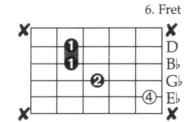

6. Fret

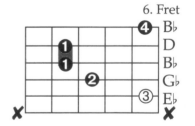

6. Fret

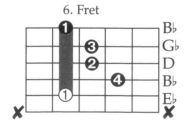

6. Fret

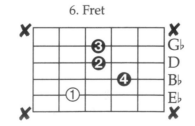

11. Fret

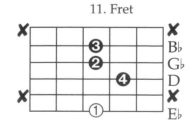

E♭
D#

E♭m add9

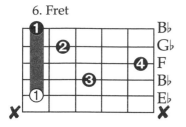
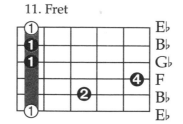
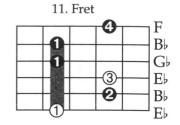

E♭m9

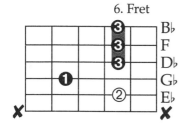
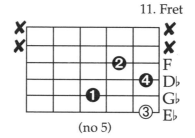
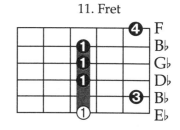

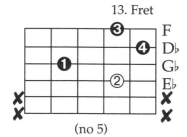

E♭m(maj9)

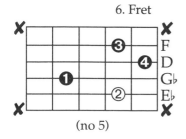
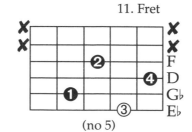
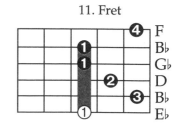

E♭m $^6_9$

E♭
D#

6. Fret

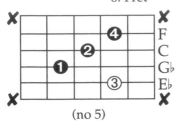

(no 5)

11. Fret

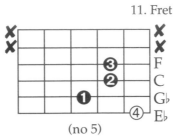

(no 5)

13. Fret

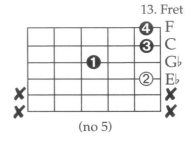

(no 5)

11. Fret

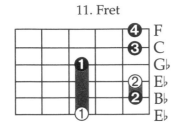

E♭m11(no9)

6. Fret

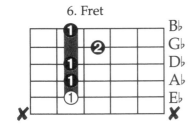

13. Fret

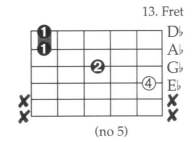

(no 5)

11. Fret

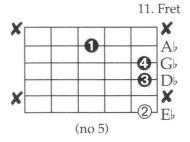

(no 5)

E♭m11

11. Fret

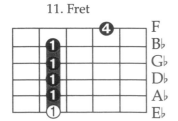

E♭7

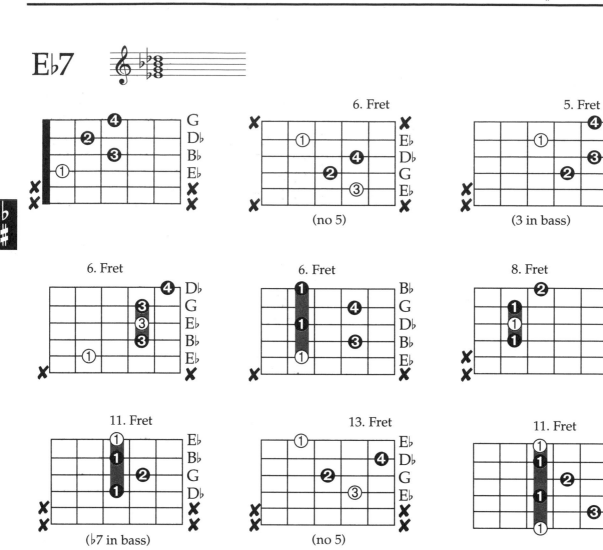

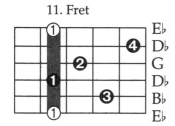

E♭9

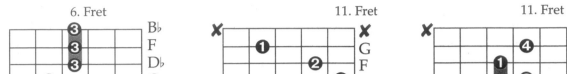

E♭
D#

6. Fret

B♭
F
D♭
G
E♭

11. Fret

G
F
D♭
E♭

(no 5)

11. Fret

B♭
F
D♭
G
E♭

11. Fret

F
B♭
G
D♭
B♭
E♭

13. Fret

F
D♭
G
E♭

(no 5)

E♭13

6. Fret

C
F
D♭
G
E♭

(no 5)

11. Fret

C
G
E♭
D♭

(no 5)

11. Fret

F
C
G
D♭
E♭

(no 5)

11. Fret

E♭
C
G
D♭

(no 5)

E♭7♭9

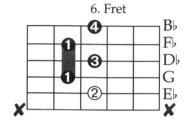

6. Fret

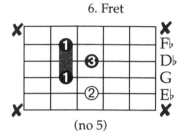

(no 5)

6. Fret

B♭
F♭
D♭
G
E♭

11. Fret

F♭
D♭
G
E♭

(no 5)

13. Fret

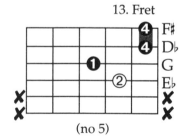

F♭
D♭
G
E♭

(no 5)

E♭7♯9

6. Fret

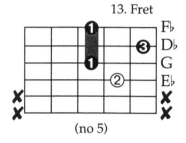

F♯
D♭
G
E♭

(no 5)

11. Fret

B♭
F♯
D♭
G
E♭

11. Fret

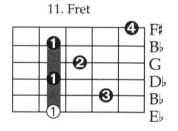

F♯
B♭
G
D♭
B♭
E♭

13. Fret

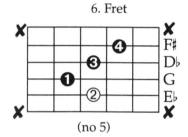

F♯
D♭
G
E♭

(no 5)

E♭13♭9

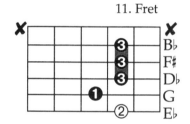

6. Fret

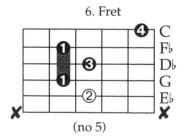

C
F♭
D♭
G
E♭

(no 5)

11. Fret

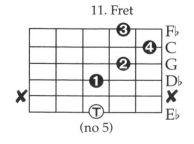

F♭
C
G
D♭
E♭

(no 5)

E♭7+

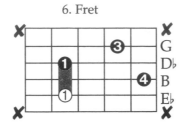

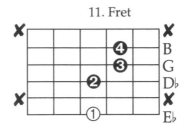

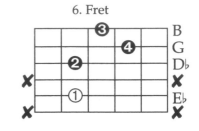

E♭
D#

6. Fret

6. Fret

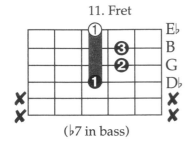

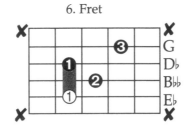

(♭7 in bass)

11. Fret

11. Fret

E♭7♭5

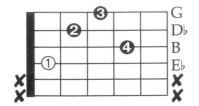

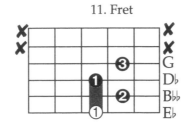

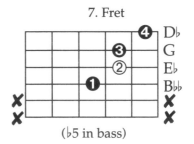

6. Fret

7. Fret

(♭5 in bass)

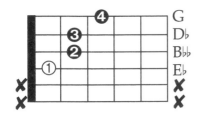

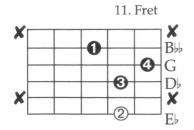

11. Fret

11. Fret

$E\flat 7{}^{\flat 9}_{\sharp 5}$

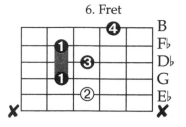 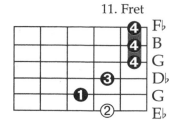

$E\flat 7{}^{\sharp 9}_{\sharp 5}$

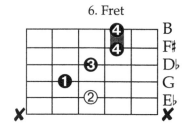 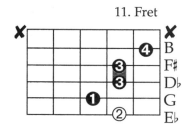

$E\flat 9\sharp 11$

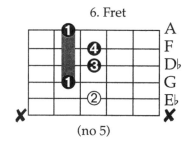 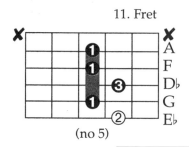

(no 5)   (no 5)

$E\flat 9+$

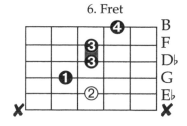 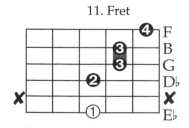

Eb7sus4

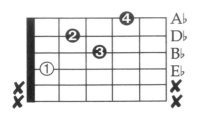
Ab
Db
Bb
Eb

6. Fret
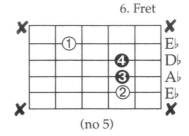
Eb
Db
Ab
Eb
(no 5)

6. Fret
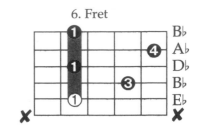
Bb
Ab
Db
Bb
Eb

8. Fret
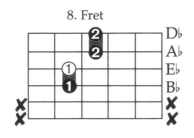
Db
Ab
Eb
Bb

11. Fret
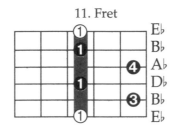
Eb
Bb
Ab
Db
Bb
Eb

Eb9sus4

F
Db
Ab
Eb
(no 5)

6. Fret
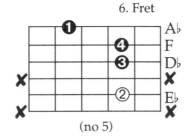
Ab
F
Db
Eb
(no 5)

6. Fret
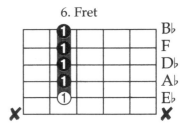
Bb
F
Db
Ab
Eb

11. Fret
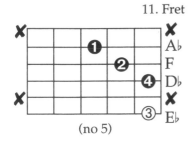
Ab
F
Db
Eb
(no 5)

Eb13sus4

6. Fret
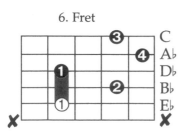
C
Ab
Db
Bb
Eb

11. Fret
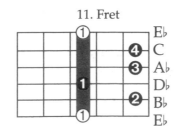
Eb
C
Ab
Db
Bb
Eb

Eb
D#

E♭°

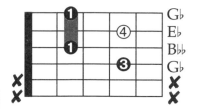 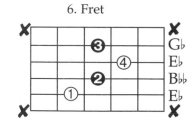 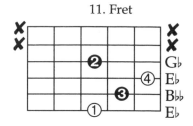

E♭/D♯

E♭m7♭5

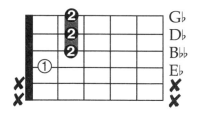 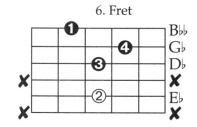 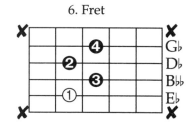

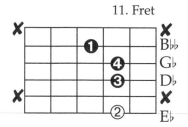 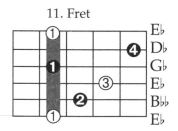

E♭°7

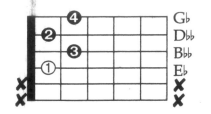
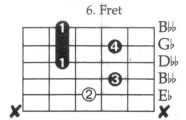
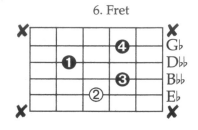

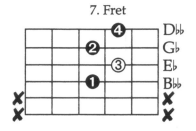
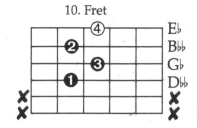
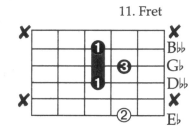

6. Fret   6. Fret

7. Fret   10. Fret   11. Fret

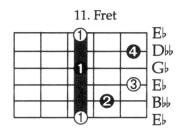

11. Fret

E♭+

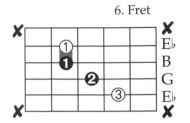 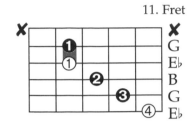 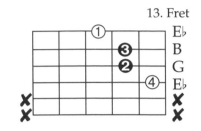

E♭sus4

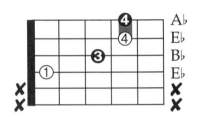 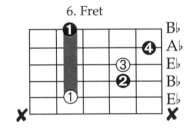 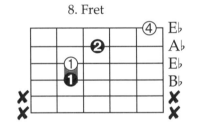

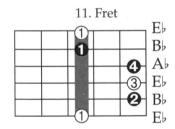

E♭sus2

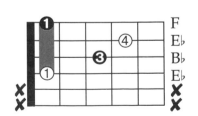 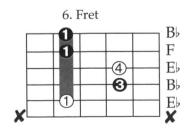 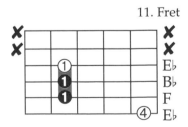

E

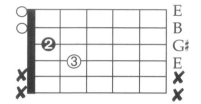

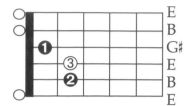

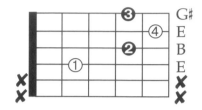

E

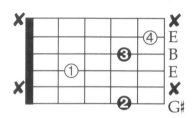

6. Fret

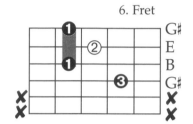

7. Fret

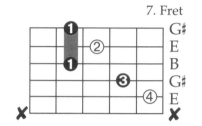

9. Fret

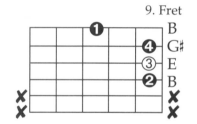

7. Fret

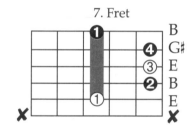

9. Fret

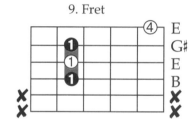

12. Fret

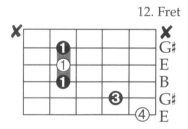

E6

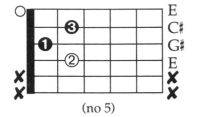

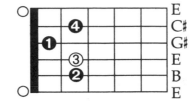

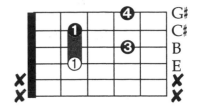

7. Fret

7. Fret

7. Fret

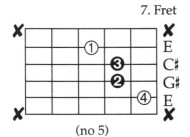

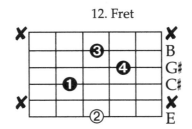

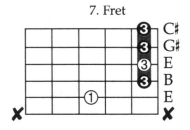

9. Fret

12. Fret

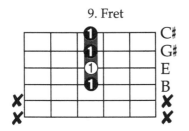

E $^6_9$

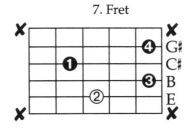

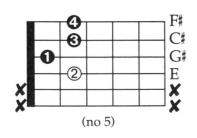

2. Fret

7. Fret

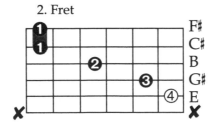

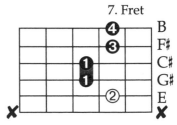

12. Fret

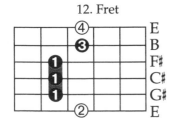

Emaj7

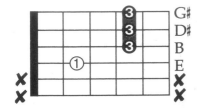

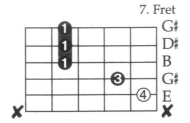
7. Fret

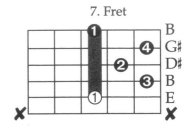
7. Fret

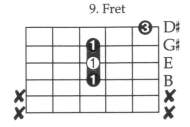
9. Fret

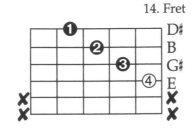
14. Fret

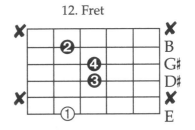
12. Fret

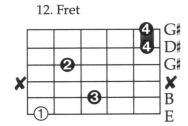
12. Fret

Emaj13

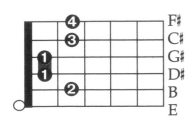

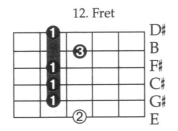
12. Fret

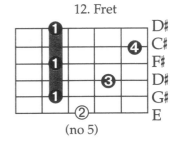
12. Fret

(no 5)

E

Emaj9

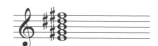

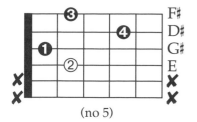
(no 5)

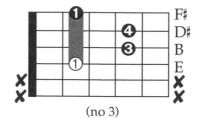
(no 3)

7. Fret
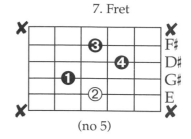
(no 5)

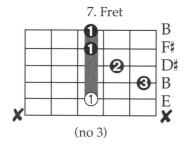
(no 3)

12. Fret
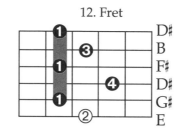

12. Fret
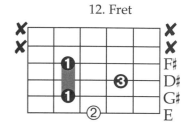

Emaj9#11

7. Fret
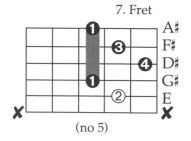
(no 5)

7. Fret
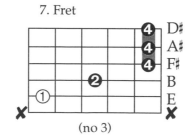
(no 3)

12. Fret
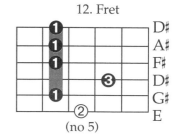
(no 5)

Emaj7+

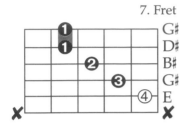

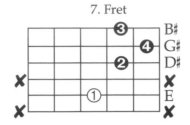

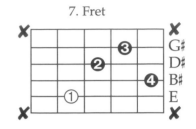

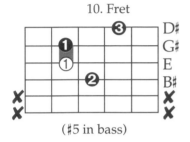

(♯5 in bass)

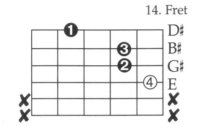

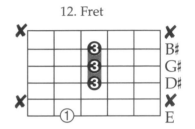

Emaj7♭5

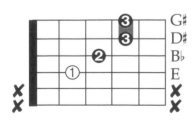

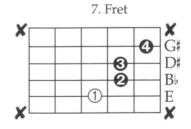

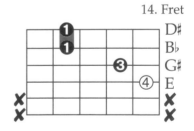

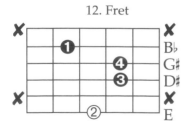

E

Emaj13(no9)

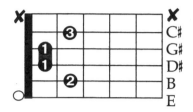

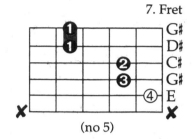

7. Fret

(no 5)

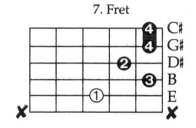

7. Fret

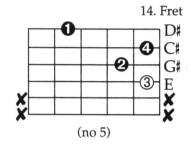

14. Fret

(no 5)

E

Eadd9

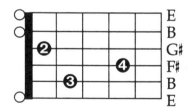

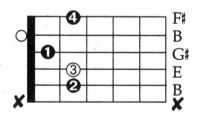

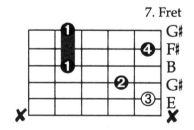

7. Fret

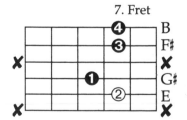

7. Fret

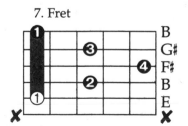

7. Fret

Em

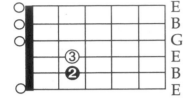

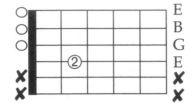

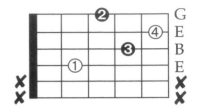

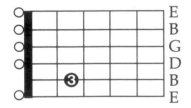

7. Fret

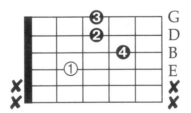

10. Fret

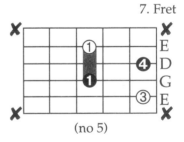

E

Em7

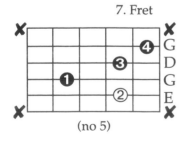

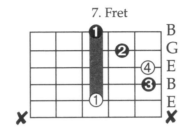

7. Fret

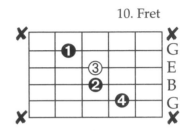

(no 5)

7. Fret

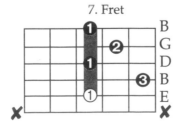

(no 5)

7. Fret

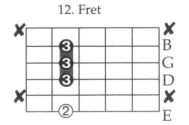

12. Fret

Em6

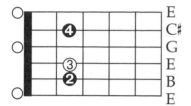
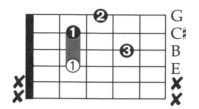
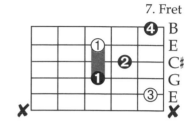

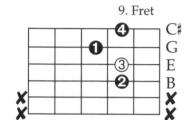
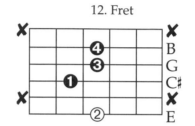

Em(maj7)

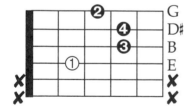
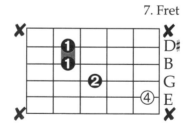
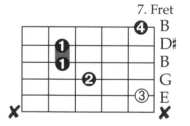

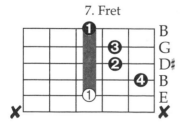
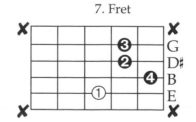
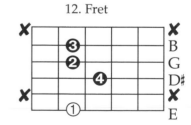

Em add9

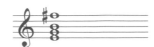

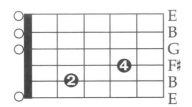

7. Fret

Em9

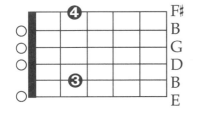

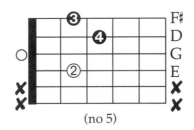

(no 5)

7. Fret

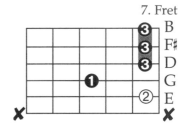

12. Fret

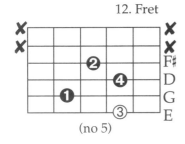

(no 5)

Em(maj9)

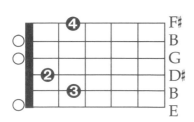

7. Fret

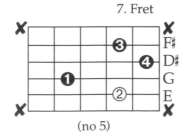

(no 5)

12. Fret

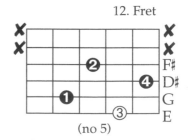

(no 5)

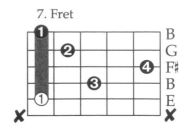

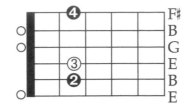

E

Em $\frac{6}{9}$

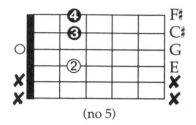
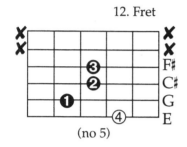

(no 5)   (no 5)   (no 5)

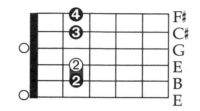

7. Fret

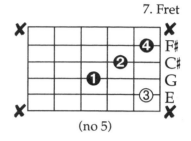

12. Fret

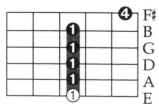

(no 5)

Em11(no9)

7. Fret   14. Fret   12. Fret

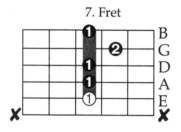
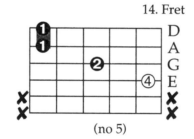
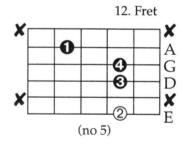

(no 5)   (no 5)

Em11

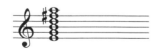

12. Fret

E7

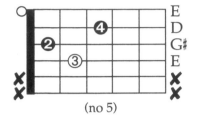

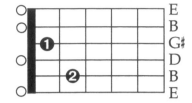

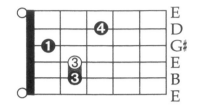

(no 5)

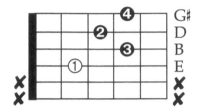

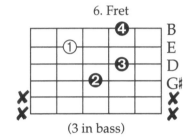

6. Fret

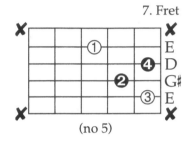

7. Fret

(3 in bass)

(no 5)

7. Fret

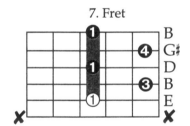

7. Fret

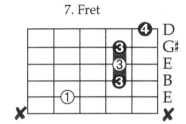

9. Fret

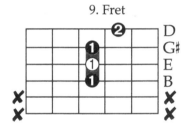

12. Fret

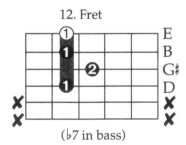

(♭7 in bass)

E

E9

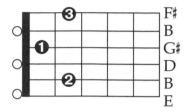

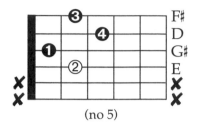

(no 5)

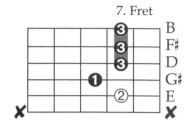

7. Fret

E

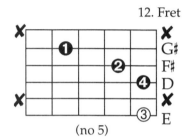

12. Fret

(no 5)

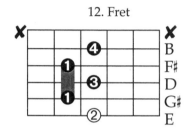

12. Fret

E13

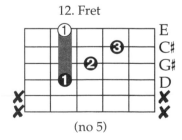

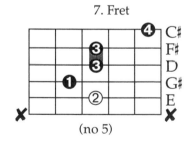

7. Fret

(no 5)

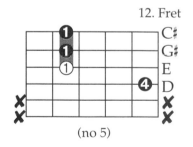

12. Fret

(no 5)

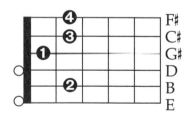

12. Fret

(no 5)

E7♭9

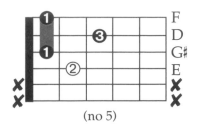 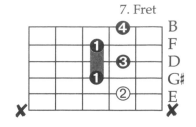

(no 5)   7. Fret (no 5)   7. Fret

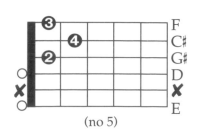

12. Fret

(no 5)

E7♯9

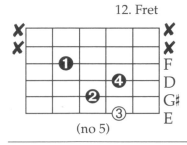 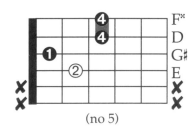 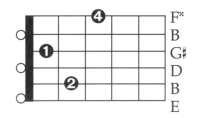 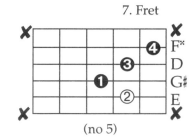

(no 5)   7. Fret (no 5)

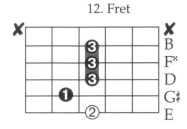

12. Fret

E13♭9

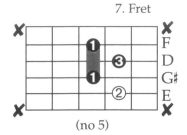 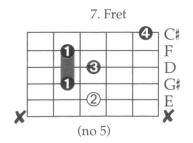

(no 5)   7. Fret (no 5)

E7+

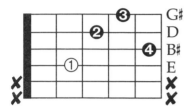
G#
D
B#
E

7. Fret

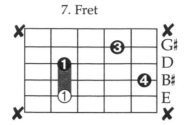
G#
D
B#
E

7. Fret

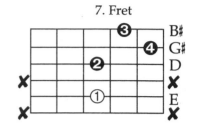
B#
G#
D
E

12. Fret

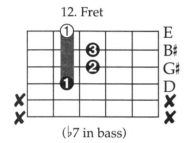
E
B#
G#
D

(♭7 in bass)

12. Fret

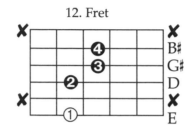
B#
G#
D
E

E7♭5

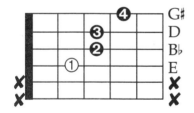
G#
D
B♭
E

7. Fret

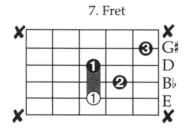
G#
D
B♭
E

8. Fret

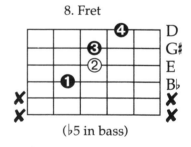
D
G#
E
B♭

(♭5 in bass)

12. Fret

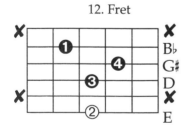
B♭
G#
D
E

12. Fret

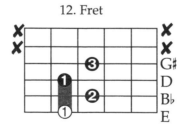
G#
D
B♭
E

E7 ♭9 ♯5

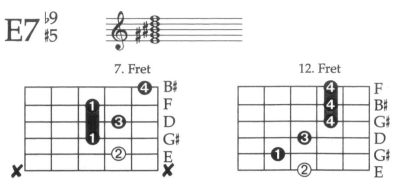

E7 ♯9 ♯5

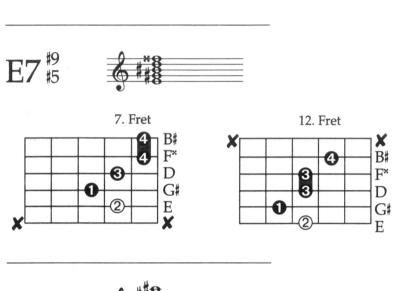

E9♯11

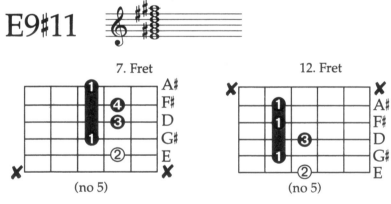

E9+

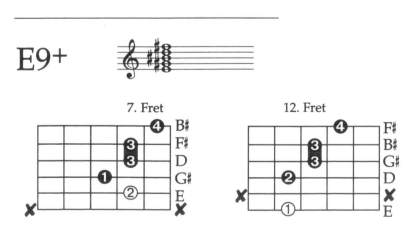

E7sus4

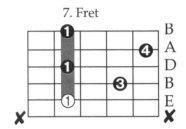

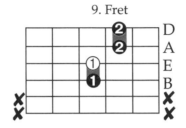

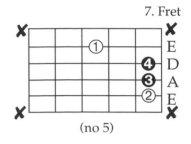

(no 5)

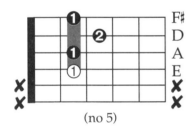

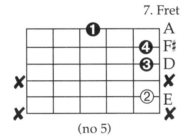

E9sus4

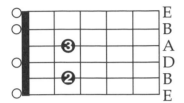

(no 5)

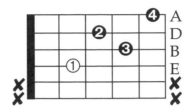

(no 5)

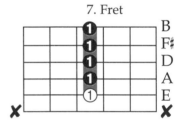

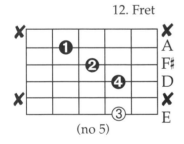

(no 5)

E13sus4

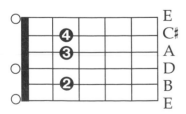

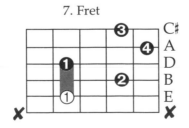

E°

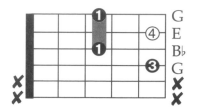

7. Fret

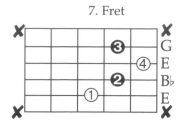

12. Fret

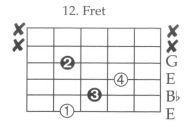

E

Em7♭5

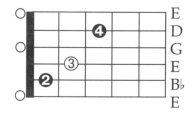

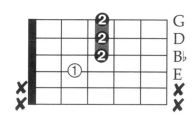

7. Fret

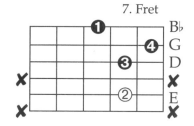

7. Fret

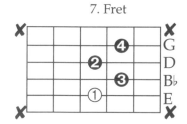

12. Fret

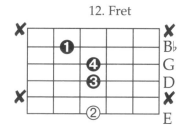

E°7

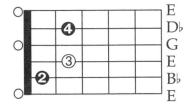
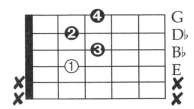
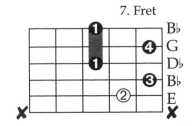

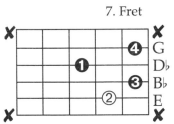
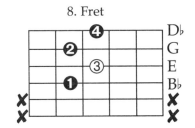
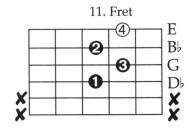

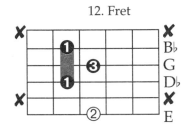

E+

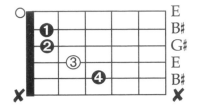

7. Fret

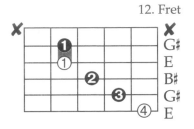

12. Fret

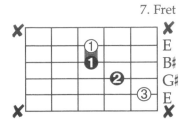

E

Esus4

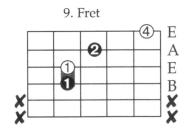

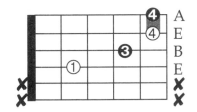

7. Fret

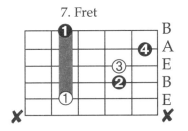

9. Fret

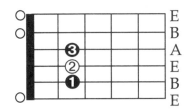

Esus2

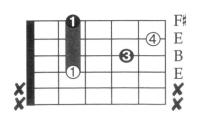

7. Fret

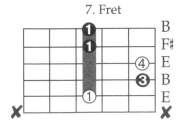

12. Fret

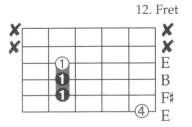

F

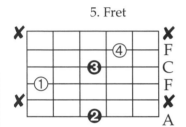

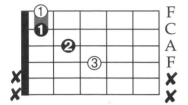

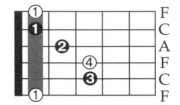

3. Fret

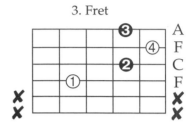

5. Fret

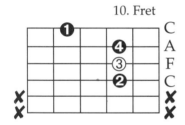

7. Fret

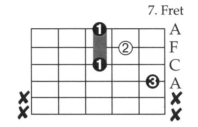

8. Fret

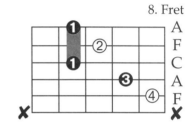

10. Fret

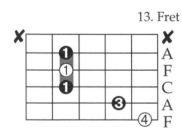

8. Fret

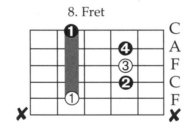

10. Fret

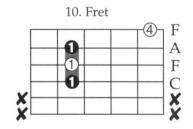

13. Fret

F6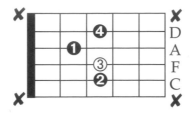

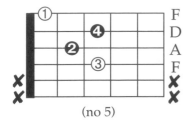
(no 5)

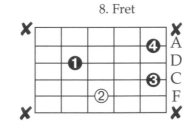

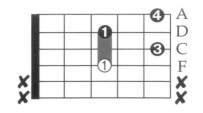

8. Fret

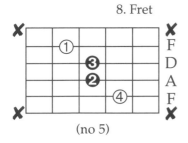
(no 5)

8. Fret

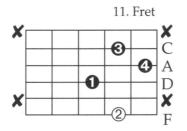

8. Fret

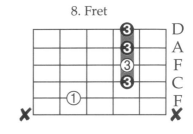

10. Fret

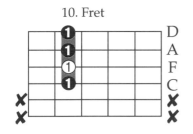

11. Fret

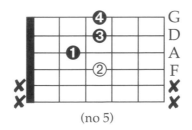

F

F $^6_9$

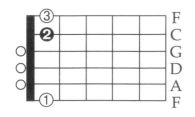
(no 5)

8. Fret

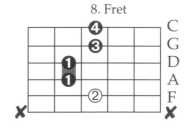

8. Fret

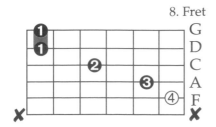

Fmaj7

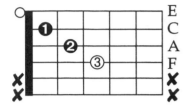 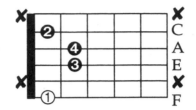 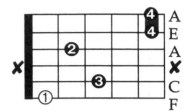

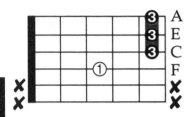 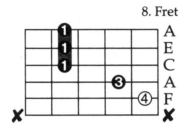 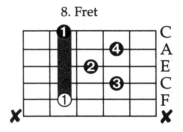

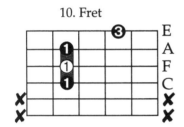

Fmaj13

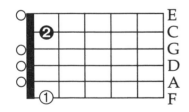 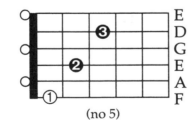 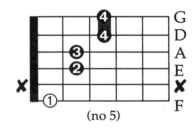

Fmaj9

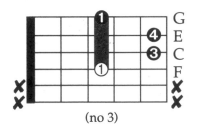

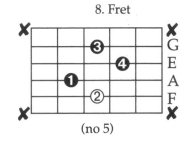
(no 5)

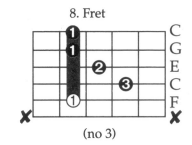
(no 5)

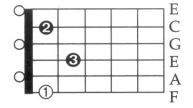
(no 3)

8. Fret

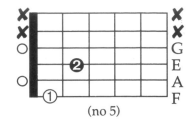
(no 5)

8. Fret

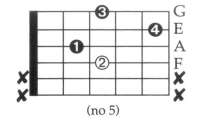
(no 3)

Fmaj9#11

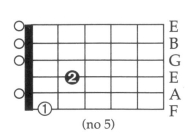
(no 5)

8. Fret

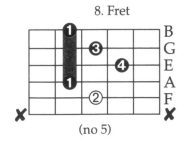
(no 5)

8. Fret

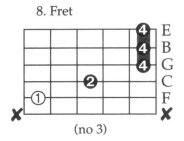
(no 3)

F

Fmaj7+

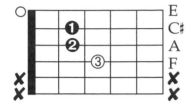
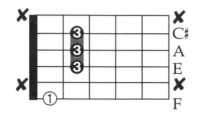
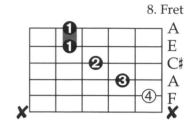

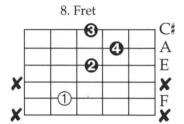
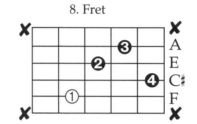
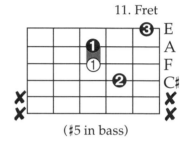

(♯5 in bass)

F

Fmaj7♭5

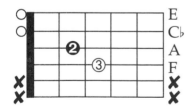
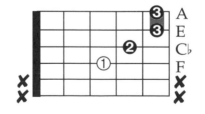
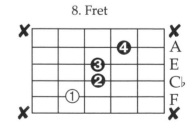

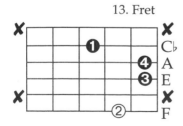

Fmaj13(no9)

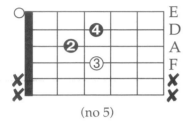

(no 5)

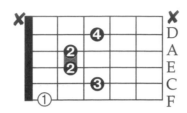

8. Fret

(no 5)

8. Fret

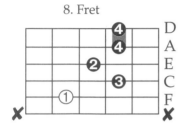

Fadd9

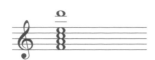

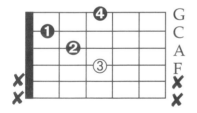

8. Fret

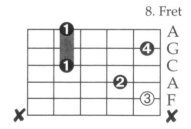

8. Fret

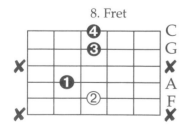

8. Fret

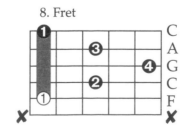

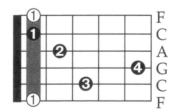

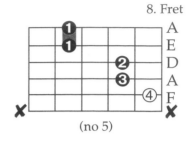

F

Fm

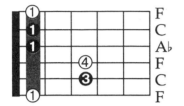

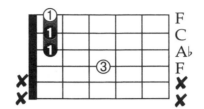

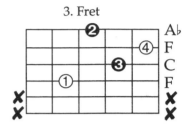

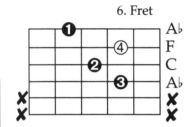

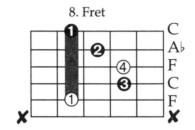

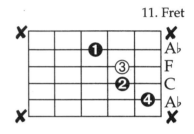

Fm7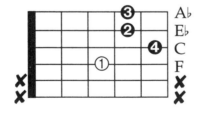

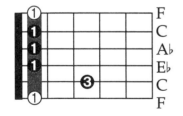

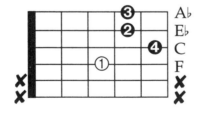

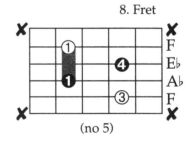

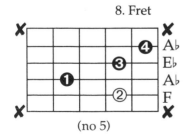

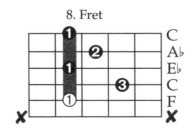

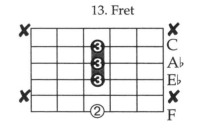

Fm6

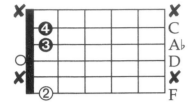

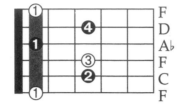

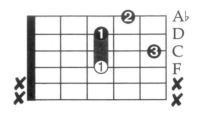

8. Fret

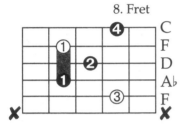

10. Fret

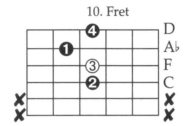

Fm(maj7)

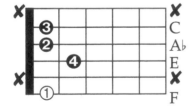

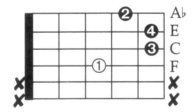

8. Fret

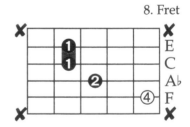

8. Fret

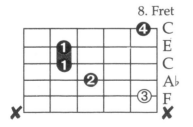

8. Fret

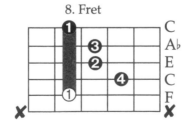

8. Fret

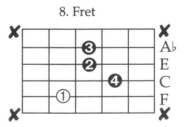

F

Fm add9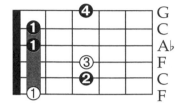

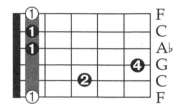

Fm9

F

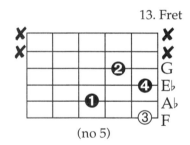

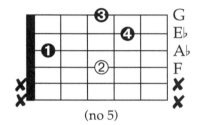

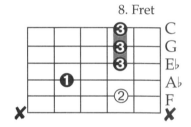

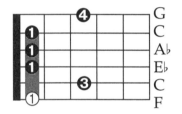

Fm(maj9)

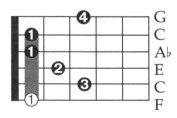

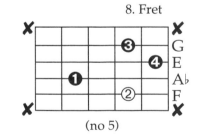

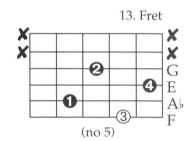

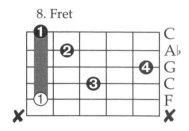

Fm $^6_9$

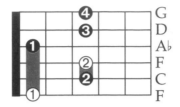

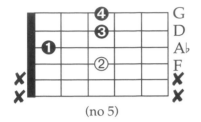

(no 5)

8. Fret

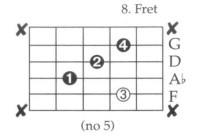

(no 5)

13. Fret

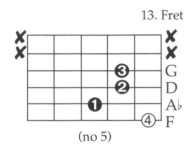

(no 5)

F

Fm11(no9)

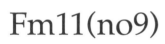

8. Fret

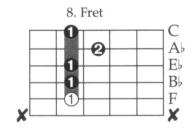

15. Fret

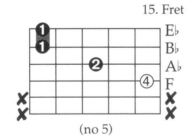

(no 5)

13. Fret

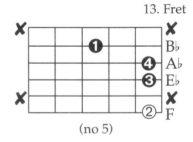

(no 5)

Fm11

13. Fret

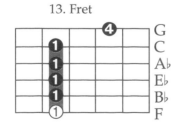

F7

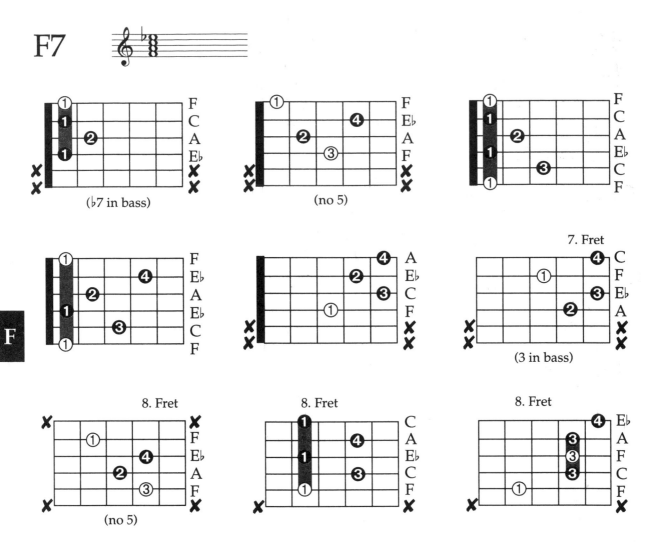

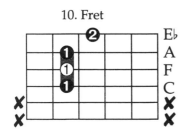

F9

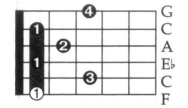

G
C
A
E♭
C
F

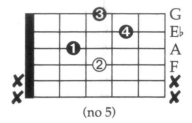

G
E♭
A
F

(no 5)

8. Fret

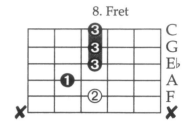

C
G
E♭
A
F

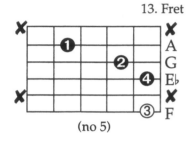

13. Fret

A
G
E♭
F

(no 5)

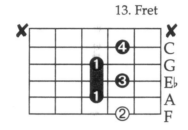

13. Fret

C
G
E♭
A
F

F

F13

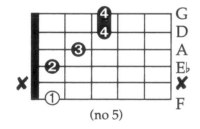

G
D
A
E♭
F

(no 5)

8. Fret

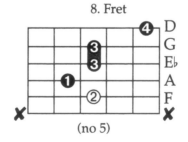

D
G
E♭
A
F

(no 5)

13. Fret

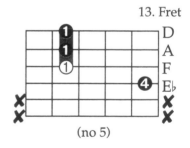

D
A
F
E♭

(no 5)

13. Fret

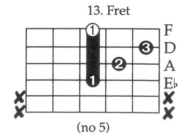

F
D
A
E♭

(no 5)

F7♭9

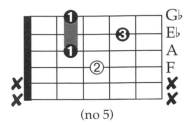

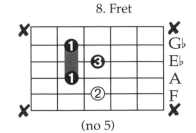

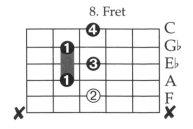

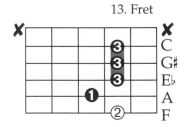

F7♯9

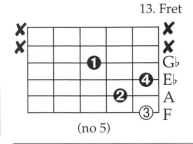

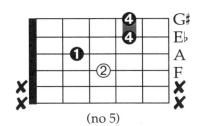

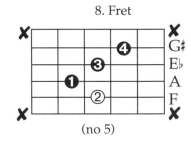

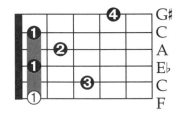

F13♭9

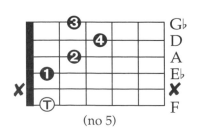

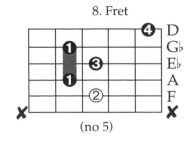

F7+

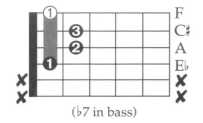

(♭7 in bass)

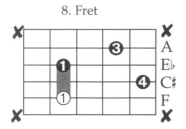

3. Fret

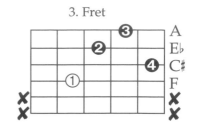

8. Fret

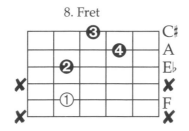

8. Fret

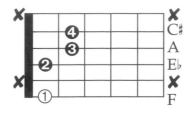

F7♭5

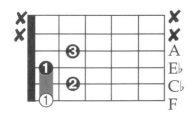

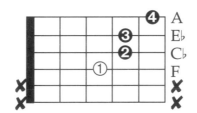

8. Fret

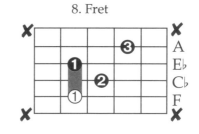

9. Fret

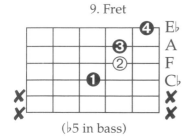

(♭5 in bass)

13. Fret

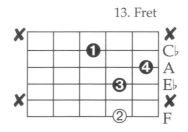

F

F7 $^{\flat9}_{\sharp5}$

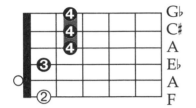   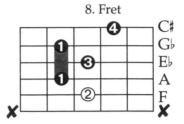

F7 $^{\sharp9}_{\sharp5}$

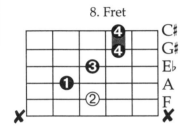   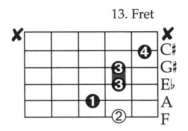

F9#11

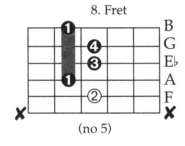   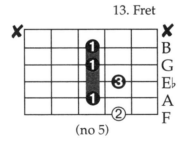

F9+

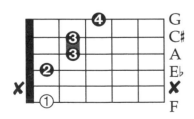   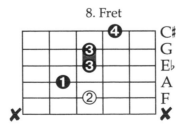

F7sus4

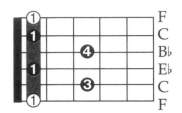

F
C
Bb
Eb
C
F

3. Fret

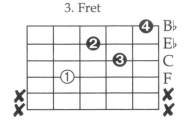

Bb
Eb
C
F

8. Fret

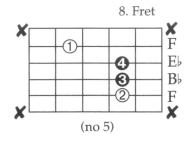

F
Eb
Bb
F

(no 5)

8. Fret

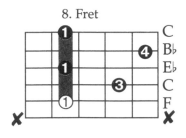

C
Bb
Eb
C
F

10. Fret

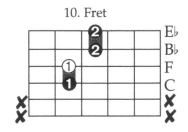

Eb
Bb
F
C

F9sus4

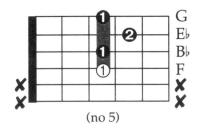

G
Eb
Bb
F

(no 5)

8. Fret

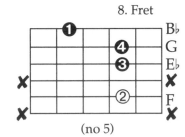

Bb
G
Eb
F

(no 5)

8. Fret

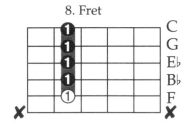

C
G
Eb
Bb
F

13. Fret

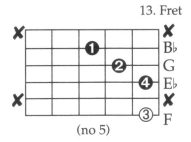

Bb
G
Eb
F

(no 5)

F13sus4

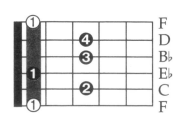

F
D
Bb
Eb
C
F

8. Fret

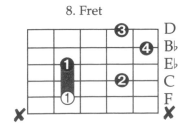

D
Bb
Eb
C
F

F°

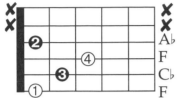

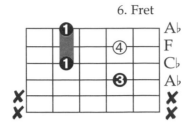

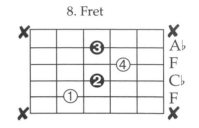

Fm7♭5

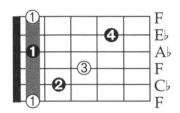

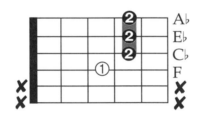

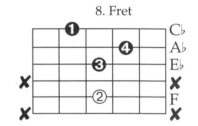

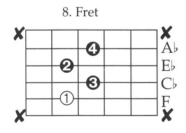

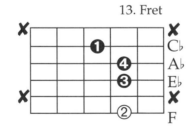

F°7

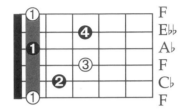

F
E♭♭
A♭
F
C♭
F

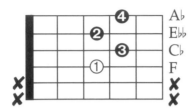

A♭
E♭♭
C♭
F

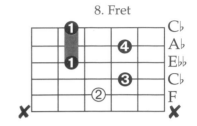

8. Fret

C♭
A♭
E♭♭
C♭
F

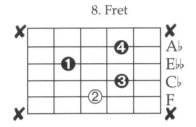

8. Fret

A♭
E♭♭
C♭
F

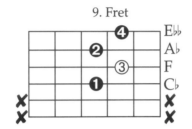

9. Fret

E♭♭
A♭
F
C♭

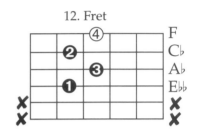

12. Fret

F
C♭
A♭
E♭♭

F

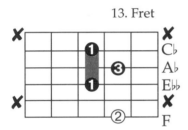

13. Fret

C♭
A♭
E♭♭
F

F+

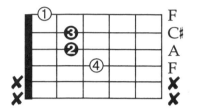

8. Fret

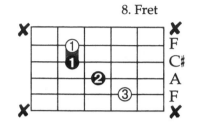

13. Fret

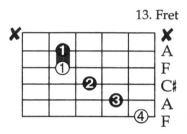

Fsus4

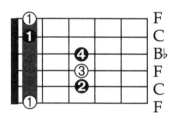

3. Fret

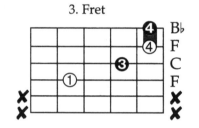

8. Fret

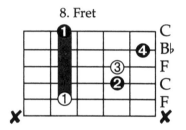

10. Fret

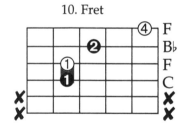

Fsus2

3. Fret

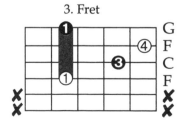

8. Fret

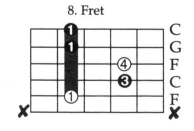

13. Fret

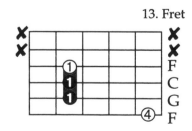

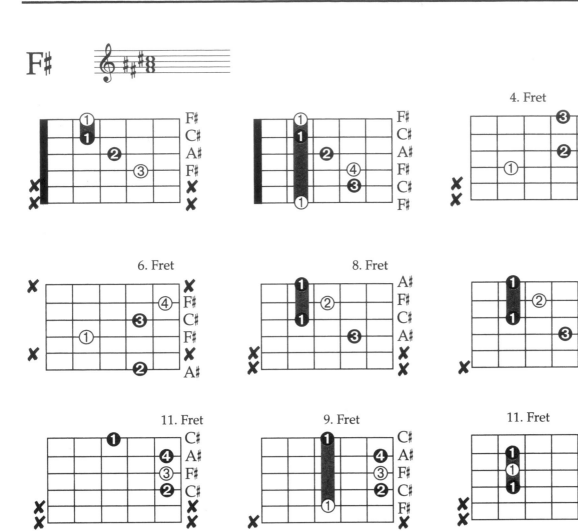

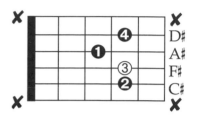

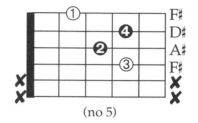

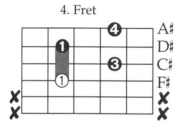

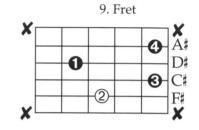

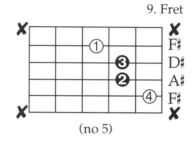

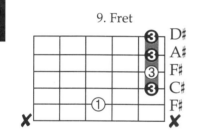

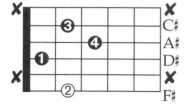

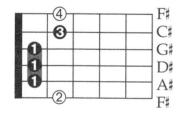

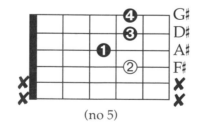

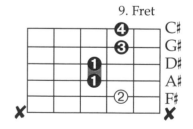

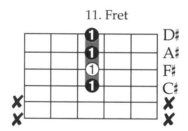

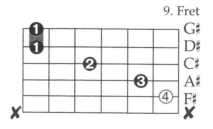

F#maj7

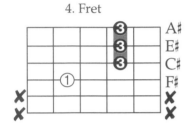 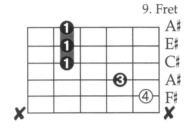 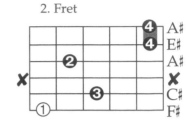

2. Fret

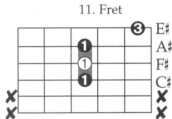 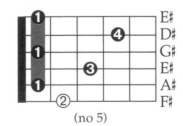 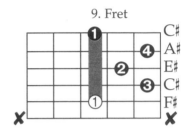

4. Fret   9. Fret   9. Fret

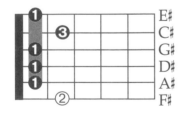

11. Fret

F#
Gb

F#maj13

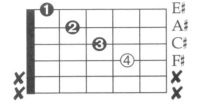 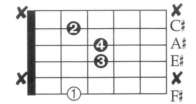 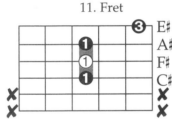

(no 5)   (no 5)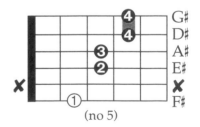

F#maj9

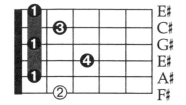

E#
C#
G#
E#
A#
F#

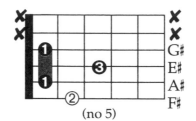

×
×
G#
E#
A#
F#

(no 5)

4. Fret

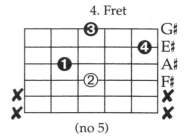

G#
E#
A#
F#
×
×

(no 5)

4. Fret

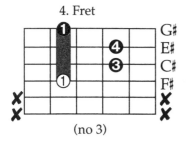

G#
E#
C#
F#
×
×

(no 3)

9. Fret

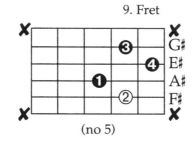

G#
E#
A#
F#

(no 5)

9. Fret

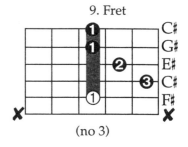

C#
G#
E#
C#
F#
×

(no 3)

F#maj9#11

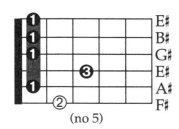

E#
B#
G#
E#
A#
F#

(no 5)

9. Fret

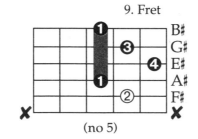

B#
G#
E#
A#
F#

(no 5)

9. Fret

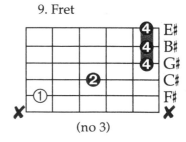

E#
B#
G#
C#
F#

(no 3)

F#maj7+

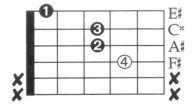

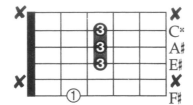

9. Fret

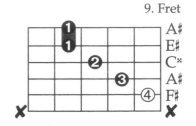

9. Fret

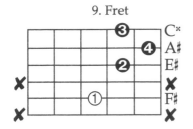

9. Fret

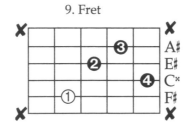

12. Fret

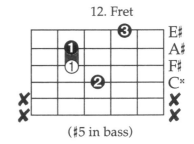

(#5 in bass)

F#maj7b5

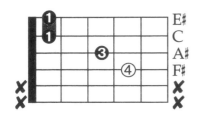

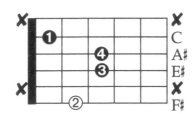

4. Fret

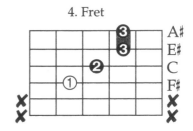

9. Fret

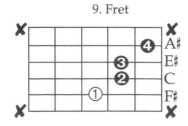

F#maj13(no9)

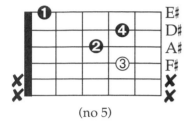

(no 5)

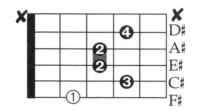

9. Fret

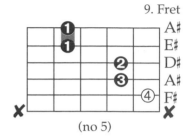

(no 5)

9. Fret

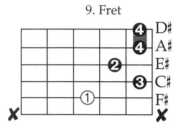

F#add9

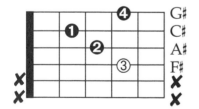

2. Fret

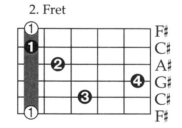

9. Fret

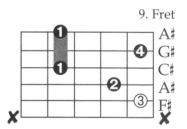

9. Fret

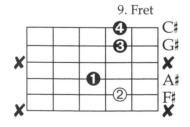

9. Fret

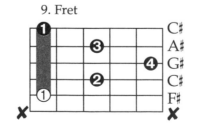

F#m

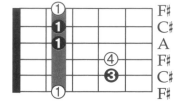

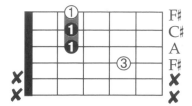

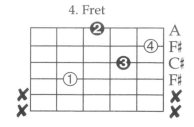

4. Fret

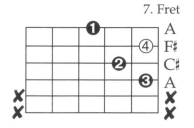

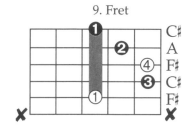

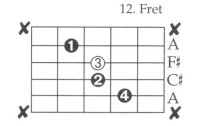

7. Fret 9. Fret 12. Fret

F#
Gb

F#m7

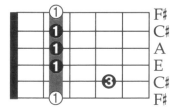

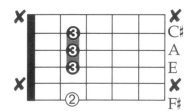

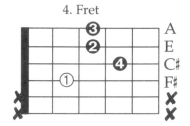

4. Fret

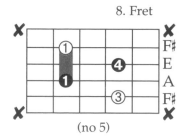

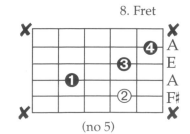

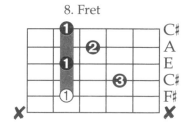

8. Fret 8. Fret 8. Fret

(no 5) (no 5)

F#m6

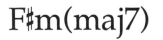

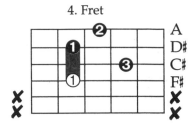

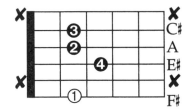
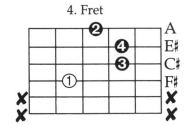

F#m(maj7)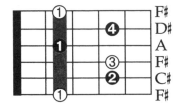

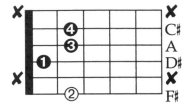
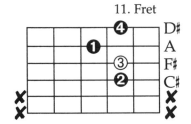
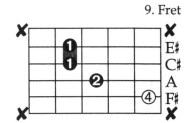

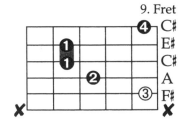
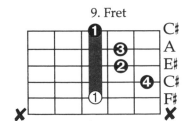
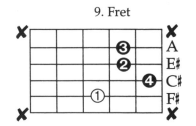

F#m add9

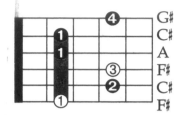

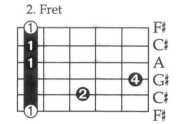

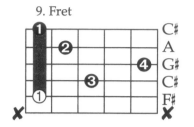

F#m9

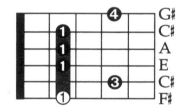

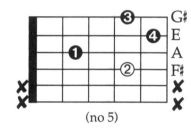

(no 5)

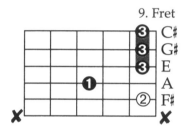

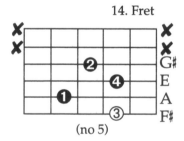

(no 5)

F#m(maj9)

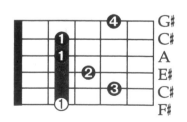

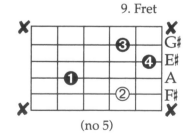

(no 5)

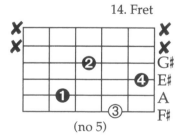

(no 5)

F#m $^6_9$

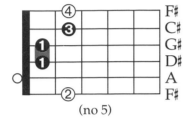
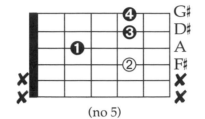
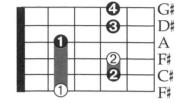

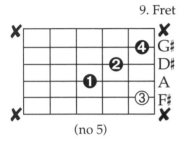

F#
G♭

F#m11(no9)

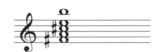

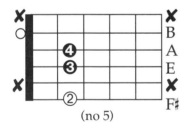
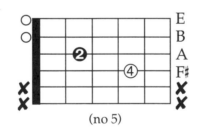
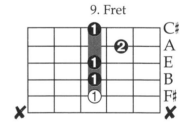

F#m11

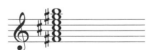

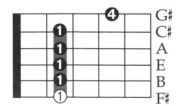

F#7

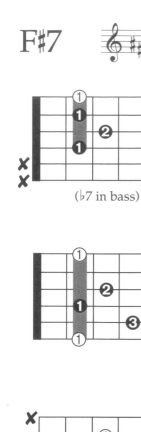

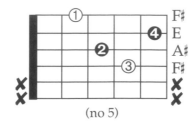

(♭7 in bass)

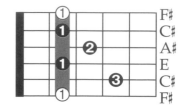

(no 5)

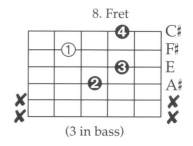

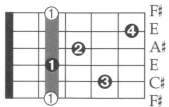

4. Fret

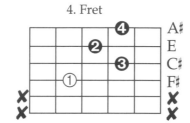

8. Fret

9. Fret

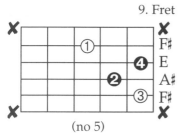

(no 5)

9. Fret

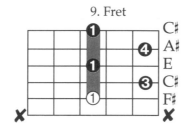

9. Fret

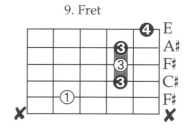

11. Fret

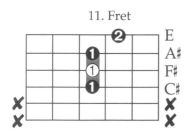

F#
G♭

F♯9

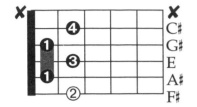

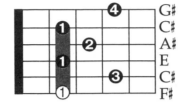

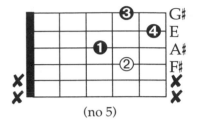

(no 5)

9. Fret

14. Fret

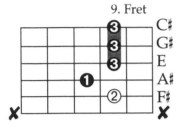

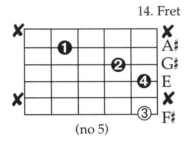

(no 5)

F♯
G♭

F♯13

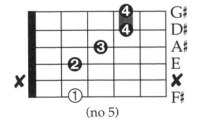

(no 5)

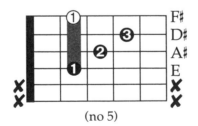

(no 5)

9. Fret

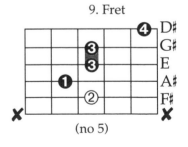

(no 5)

14. Fret

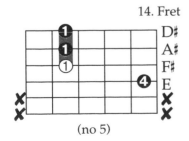

(no 5)

F#7♭9

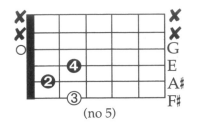
(no 5)

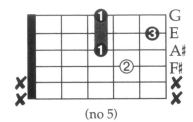
(no 5)

9. Fret

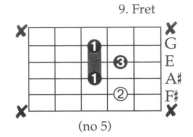
(no 5)

9. Fret

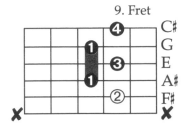

F#7#9

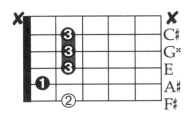

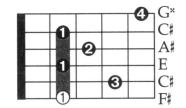

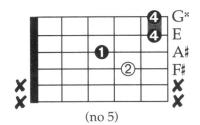
(no 5)

9. Fret

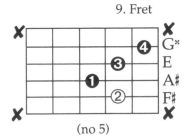
(no 5)

F#13♭9

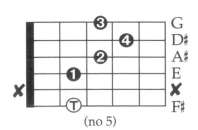
(no 5)

9. Fret

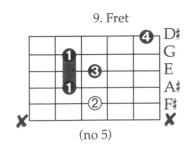
(no 5)

F♯7+

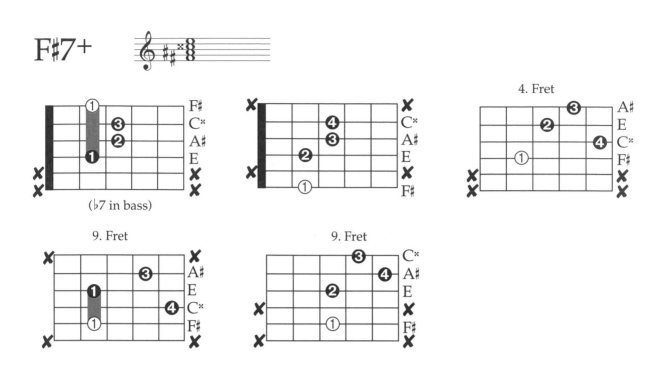

F♯7♭5

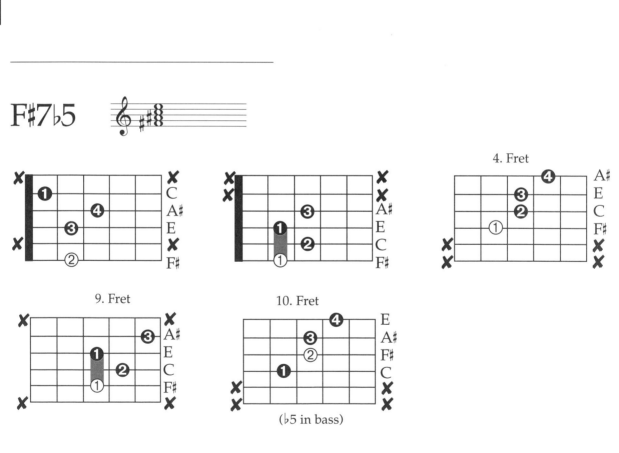

F#7 ♭9 #5

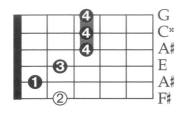

9. Fret

F7 #9 #5

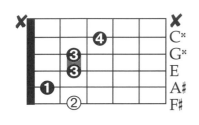

9. Fret

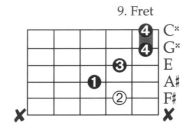

F#9#11

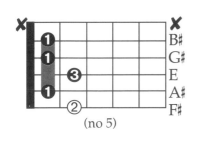
(no 5)

9. Fret

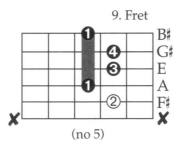
(no 5)

F#9+

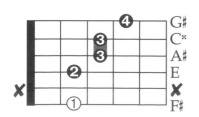

9. Fret

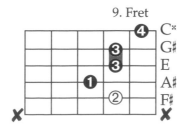

F#7sus4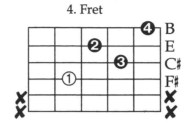

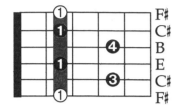

4. Fret

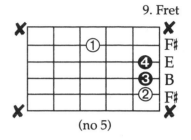

9. Fret

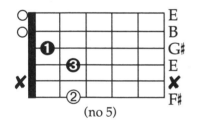

9. Fret

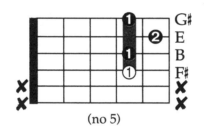

11. Fret

F#9sus4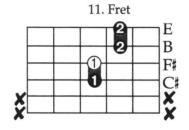

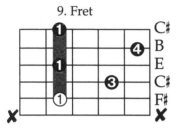

(no 5)

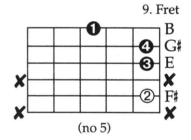

9. Fret

(no 5)

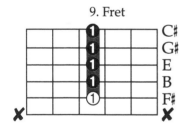

9. Fret

F#13sus4

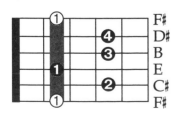

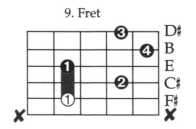

9. Fret

F#°

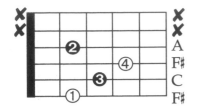

7. Fret

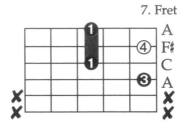

9. Fret

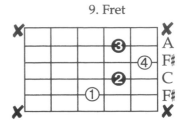

F#m7b5

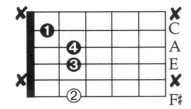

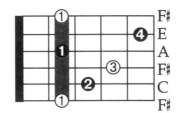

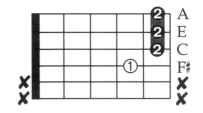

9. Fret

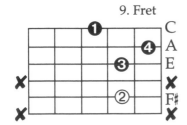

9. Fret

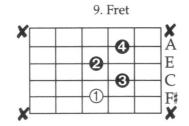

F#
Gb

F♯°7

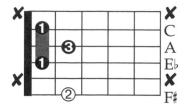

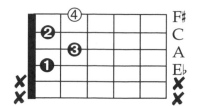

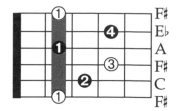

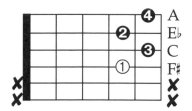

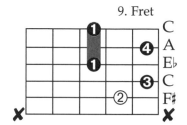

9. Fret

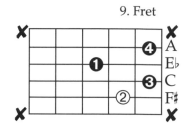

9. Fret

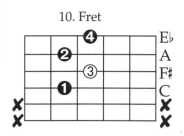

10. Fret

F#+

 9. Fret 14. Fret

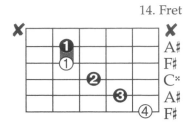

F#sus4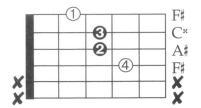

F#
Gb

4. Fret 9. Fret

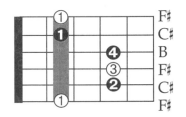 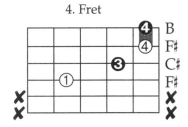 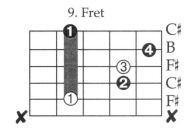

11. Fret

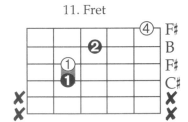

F#sus2

4. Fret 9. Fret 14. Fret

 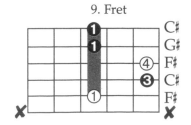 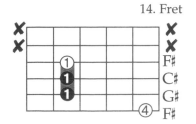

G

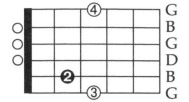

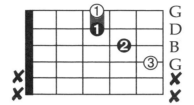

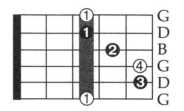

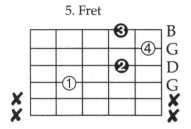

5. Fret

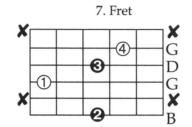

7. Fret

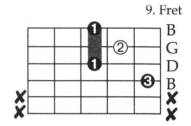

9. Fret

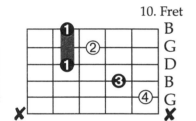

10. Fret

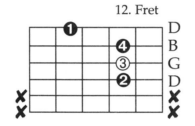

12. Fret

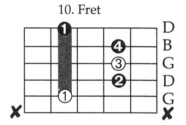

10. Fret

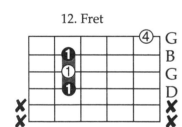

12. Fret

G6

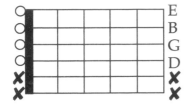

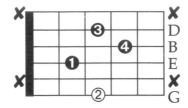

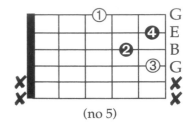

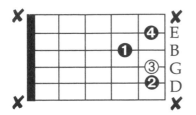

5. Fret

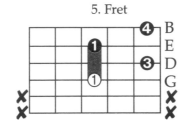

10. Fret

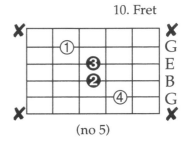

10. Fret

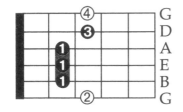

10. Fret

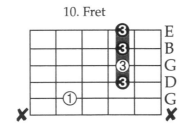

G $\frac{6}{9}$

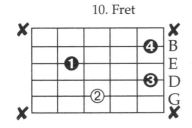

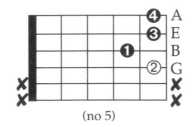

10. Fret

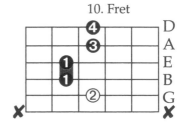

10. Fret

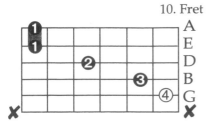

G

Gmaj7

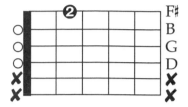
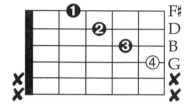
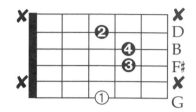

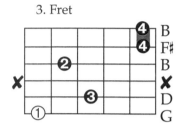
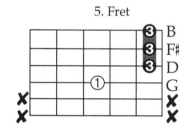
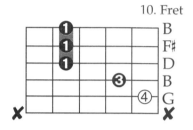

3. Fret   5. Fret   10. Fret

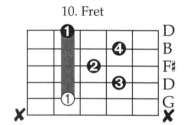

10. Fret

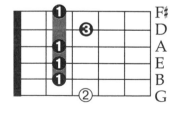

Gmaj13

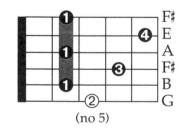
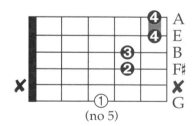

(no 5)   (no 5)

Gmaj9

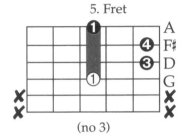
F#
D
A
F#
B
G

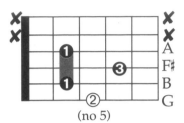
X
X
A
F#
B
G
(no 5)

5. Fret
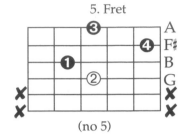
A
F#
B
G
(no 5)

5. Fret
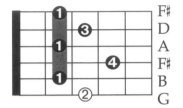
A
F#
D
G
(no 3)

10. Fret
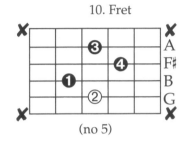
A
F#
B
G
(no 5)

10. Fret
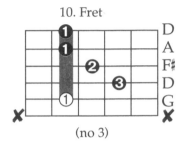
D
A
F#
D
G
(no 3)

Gmaj9#11

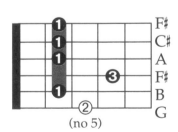
F#
C#
A
F#
B
G
(no 5)

10. Fret
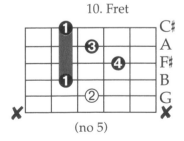
C#
A
F#
B
G
(no 5)

10. Fret
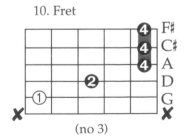
F#
C#
A
D
G
(no 3)

G

Gmaj7+

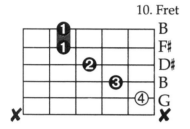
(♯5 in bass)

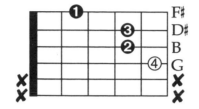

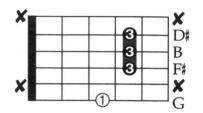

10. Fret

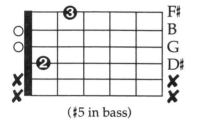

10. Fret

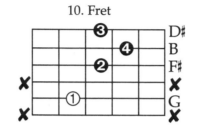

10. Fret

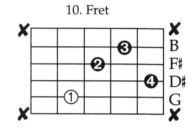

Gmaj7♭5

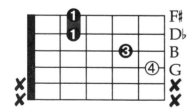

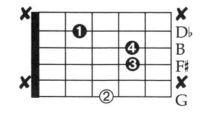

5. Fret

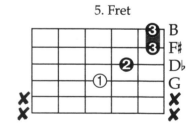

10. Fret

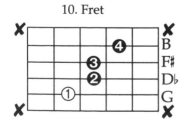

G

Gmaj13(no9)

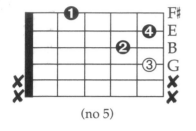

(no 5)

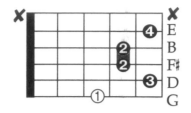

10. Fret

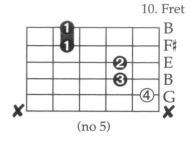

(no 5)

10. Fret

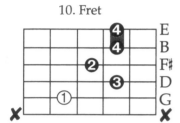

Gadd9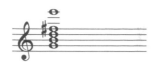

G

3. Fret

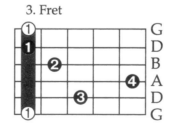

10. Fret

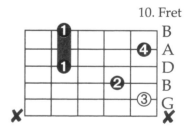

10. Fret

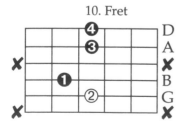

10. Fret

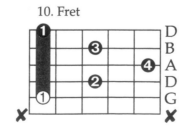

Gm

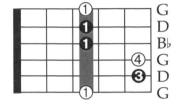
G
D
B♭
G
D
G

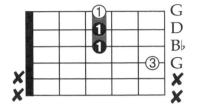
G
D
B♭
G

5. Fret

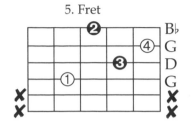
B♭
G
D
G

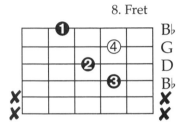
8. Fret
B♭
G
D
B♭

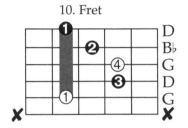
10. Fret
D
B♭
G
D
G

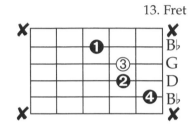
13. Fret
B♭
G
D
B♭

G

Gm7

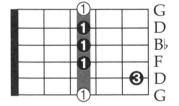
G
D
B♭
F
D
G

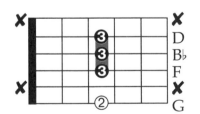
D
B♭
F
G

5. Fret

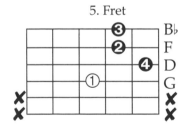
B♭
F
D
G

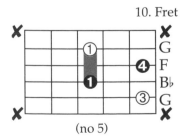
G
F
B♭
G

(no 5)

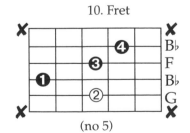
10. Fret
B♭
F
B♭
G

(no 5)

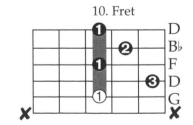
10. Fret
D
B♭
F
D
G

Gm6

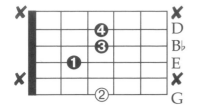 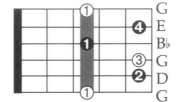 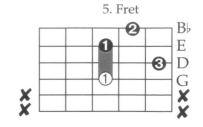

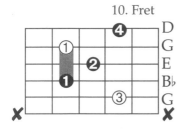 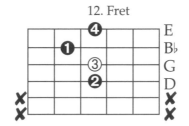

Gm(maj7)

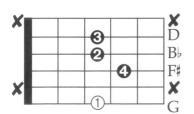 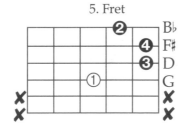 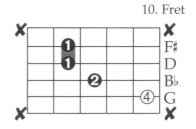

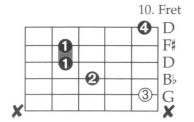 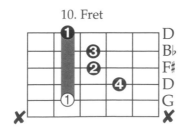 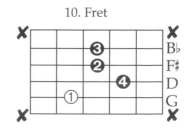

G

Gm add9

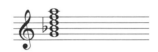

Gm9

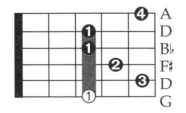

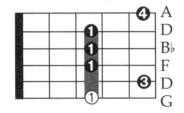

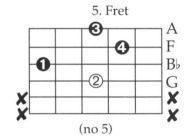

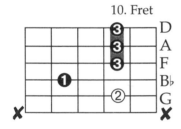

Gm(maj9)

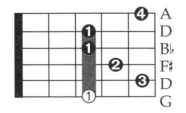

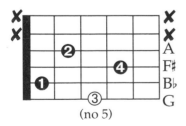

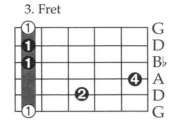

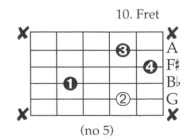

Gm $^6_9$

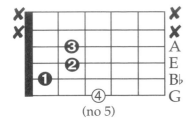
(no 5)

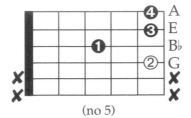
(no 5)

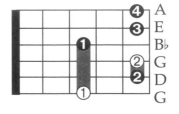

10. Fret

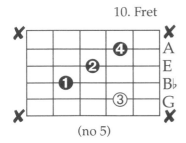
(no 5)

Gm11(no9)

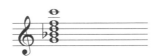

(no 5)

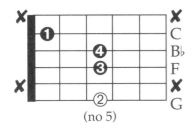
(no 5)

10. Fret

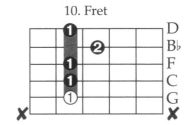

G

Gm11

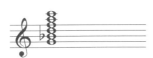

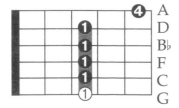

G7

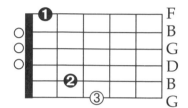
F
B
G
D
B
G

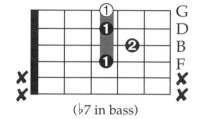
G
D
B
F

(♭7 in bass)

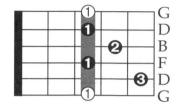
G
D
B
F
D
G

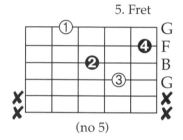
5. Fret
G
F
B
G

(no 5)

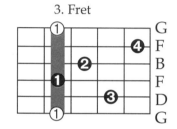
3. Fret
G
F
B
F
D
G

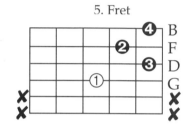
5. Fret
B
F
D
G

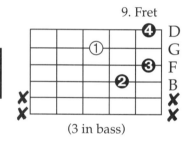
9. Fret
D
G
F
B

(3 in bass)

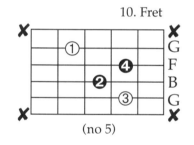
10. Fret
G
F
B
G

(no 5)

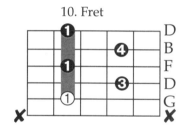
10. Fret
D
B
F
D
G

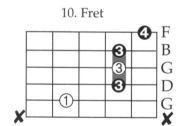
10. Fret
F
B
G
D
G

G9

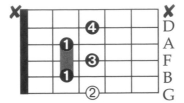

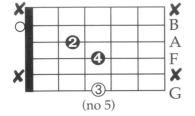

(no 5)

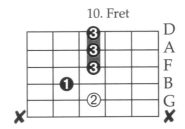

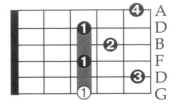

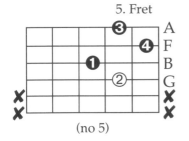

5. Fret

(no 5)

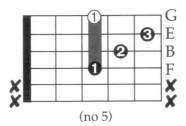

10. Fret

G13

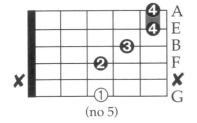

(no 5)

(no 5)

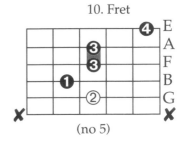

10. Fret

(no 5)

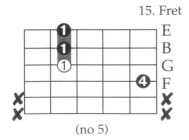

15. Fret

(no 5)

G7♭9

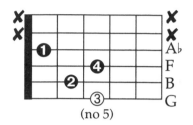
(no 5)

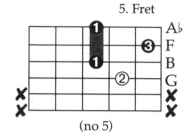
5. Fret
(no 5)

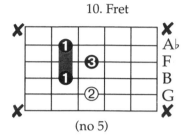
10. Fret
(no 5)

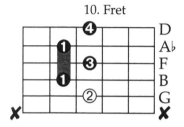
10. Fret

G7♯9

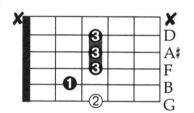

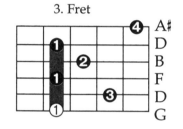
3. Fret

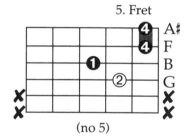
5. Fret
(no 5)

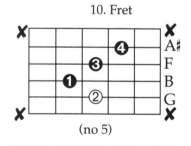
10. Fret
(no 5)

G13♭9

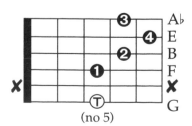
(no 5)

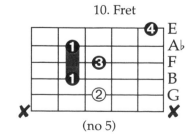
10. Fret
(no 5)

G7+

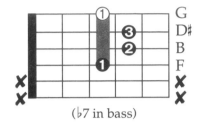

(♭7 in bass)

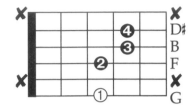

5. Fret

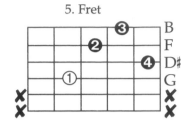

10. Fret

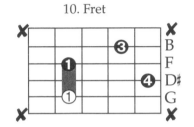

10. Fret

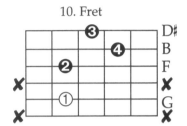

G7♭5

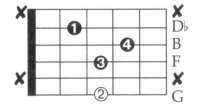

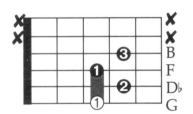

5. Fret

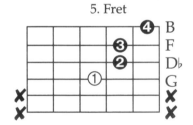

10. Fret

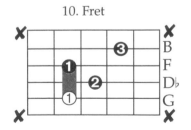

11. Fret

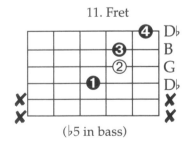

(♭5 in bass)

G7 ♭9 ♯5

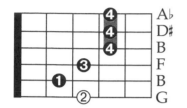

10. Fret

G7 ♯9 ♯5

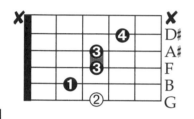

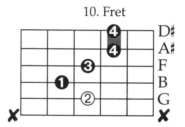

10. Fret

G

G9♯11

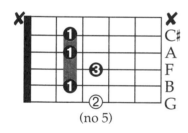

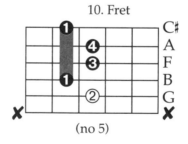

10. Fret

(no 5)   (no 5)

G9+

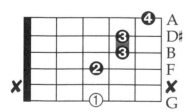

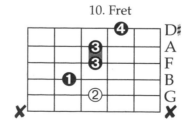

10. Fret

G7sus4

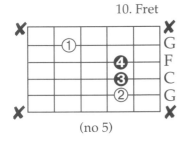 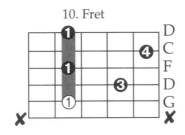 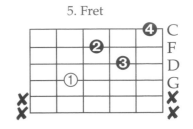

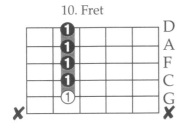
(no 5)

G9sus4

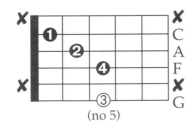
(no 5)

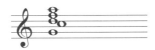

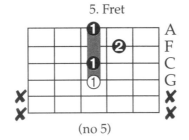
(no 5)

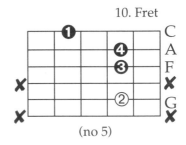
(no 5)

G

G13sus4

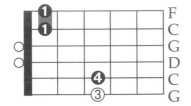

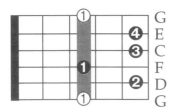 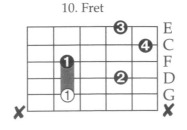

G°

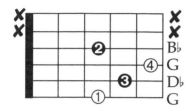 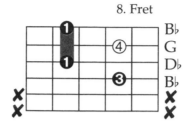 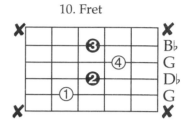

Gm7♭5

 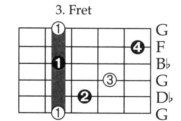 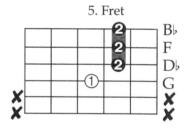

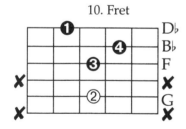 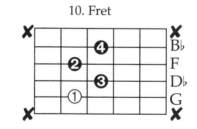

G°7

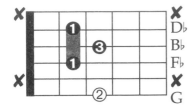

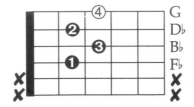

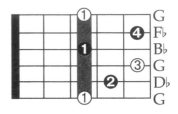

5. Fret

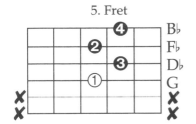

10. Fret

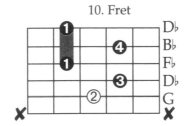

10. Fret

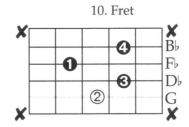

11. Fret

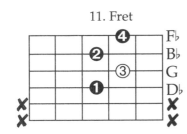

G

G+

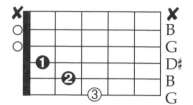
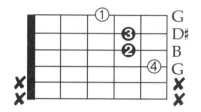
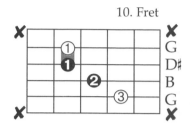

Gsus4

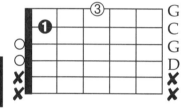
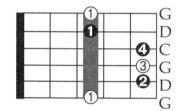
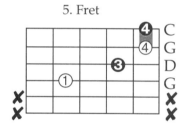

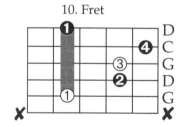

Gsus2

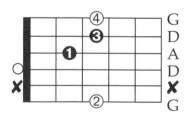
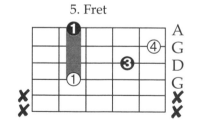
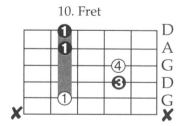

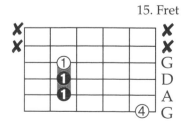

A♭

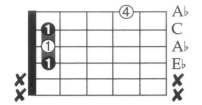

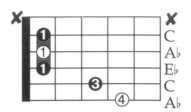

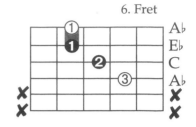

6. Fret

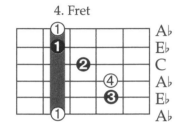

4. Fret

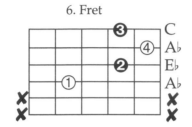

6. Fret

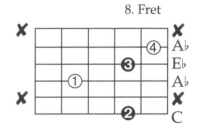

8. Fret

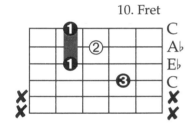

10. Fret

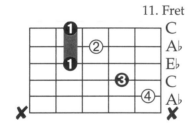

11. Fret

13. Fret

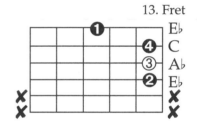

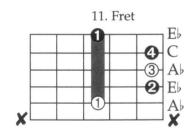

11. Fret

A♭
G♯

A♭6

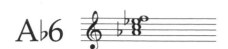

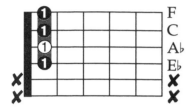

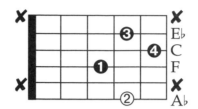

6. Fret

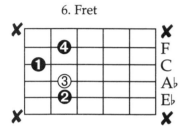

6. Fret

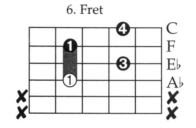

6. Fret

(no 5)

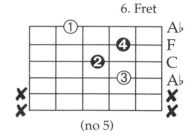

11. Fret

(no 5)

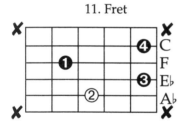

11. Fret

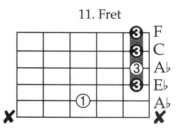

11. Fret

A♭
G♯

A♭$^6_9$

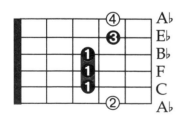

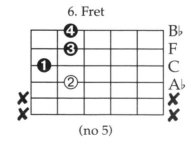

6. Fret

(no 5)

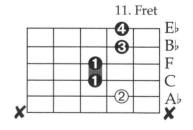

11. Fret

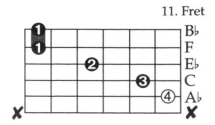

11. Fret

A♭maj7

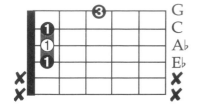

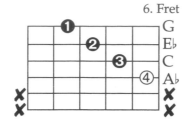

6. Fret

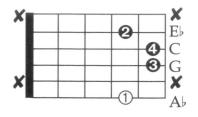

4. Fret

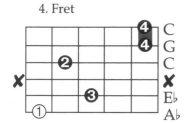

6. Fret

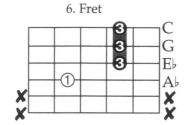

11. Fret

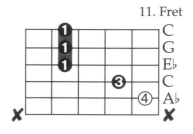

11. Fret

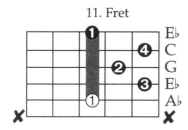

A♭
G♯

A♭maj13

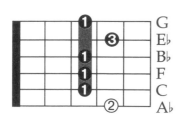

4. Fret

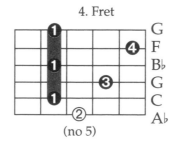

(no 5)

4. Fret

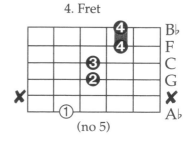

(no 5)

Abmaj9

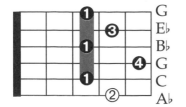

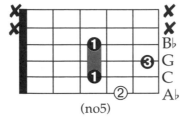

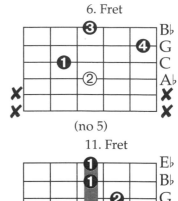

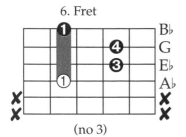

(no5)

(no 5)

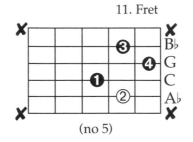

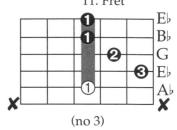

(no 3)

(no 5)

(no 3)

Ab
G#

Abmaj9#11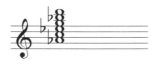

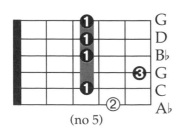

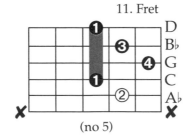

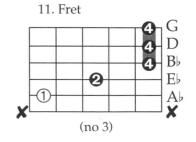

(no 5)

(no 5)

(no 3)

A♭maj7+

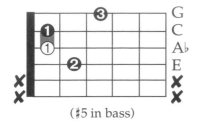

(#5 in bass)

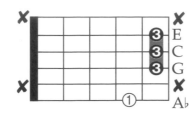

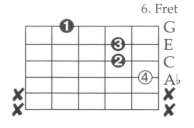
6. Fret

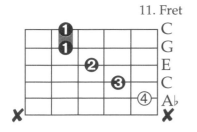
11. Fret

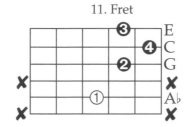
11. Fret

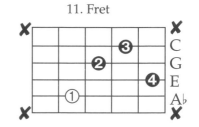
11. Fret

A♭maj7♭5

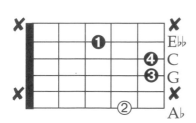

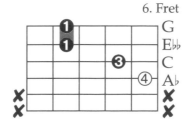
6. Fret

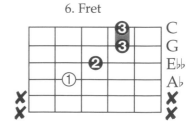
6. Fret

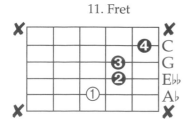
11. Fret

A♭maj13(no9)

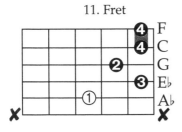

6. Fret

G
F
C
A♭

(no 5)

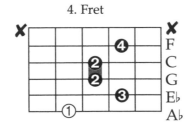

4. Fret

F
C
G
E♭
A♭

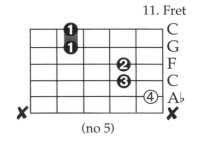

11. Fret

C
G
F
C
A♭

(no 5)

11. Fret

F
C
G
E♭
A♭

A♭add9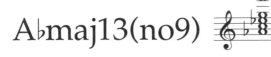

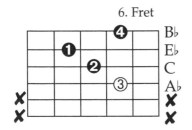

6. Fret

B♭
E♭
C
A♭

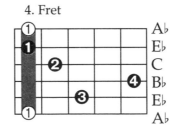

4. Fret

A♭
E♭
C
B♭
E♭
A♭

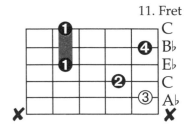

11. Fret

C
B♭
E♭
C
A♭

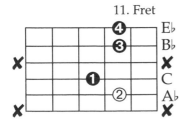

11. Fret

E♭
B♭
C
A♭

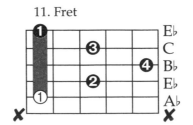

11. Fret

E♭
C
B♭
E♭
A♭

A♭m

4. Fret
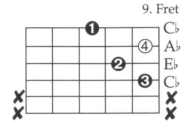

6. Fret
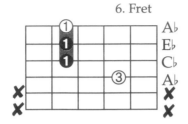

6. Fret
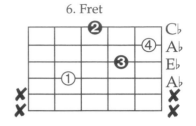

9. Fret

11. Fret
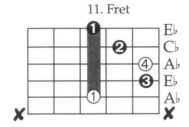

14. Fret
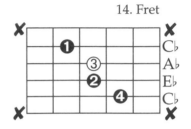

A♭
G♯

A♭m7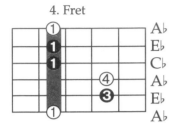

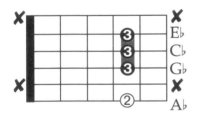

4. Fret
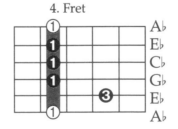

6. Fret
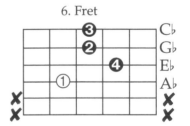

11. Fret
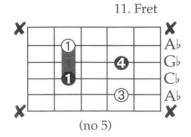
(no 5)

11. Fret
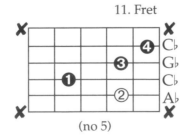
(no 5)

11. Fret
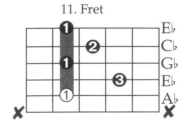

A♭m6

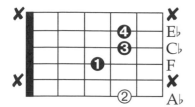

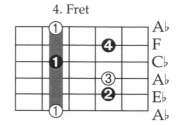

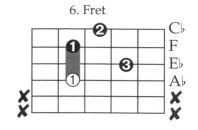

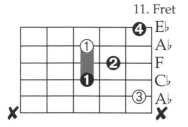

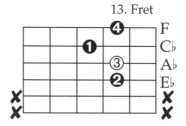

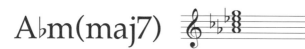

A♭m(maj7)

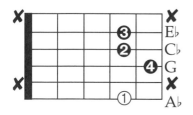

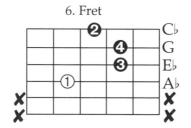

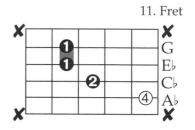

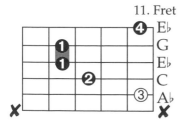

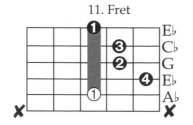

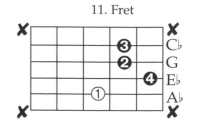

A♭m add9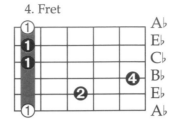

4. Fret
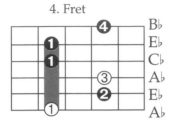

4. Fret
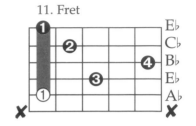

11. Fret
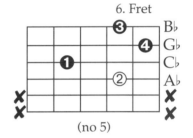

A♭m9

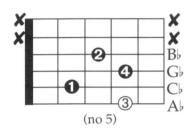
(no 5)

4. Fret
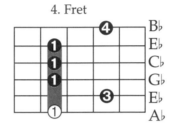

6. Fret

(no 5)

11. Fret
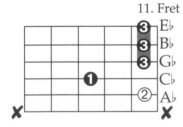

A♭
G♯

A♭m(maj9)

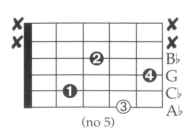
(no 5)

4. Fret
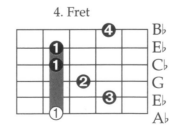

11. Fret
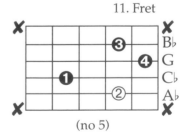
(no 5)

Abm 6/9

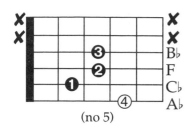

(no 5)

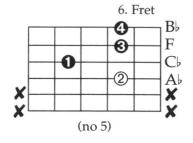

(no 5)

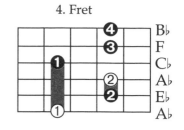

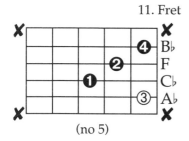

(no 5)

Abm11(no9)

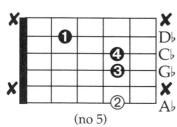

(no 5)

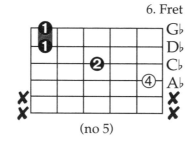

(no 5)

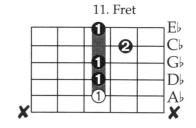

Abm11

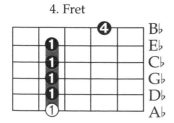

A♭7

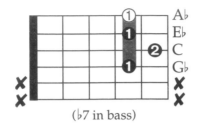

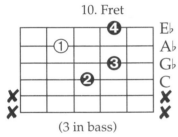

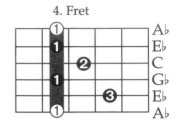

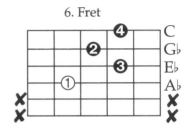

(♭7 in bass)

4. Fret

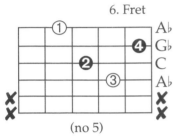

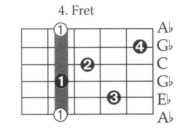

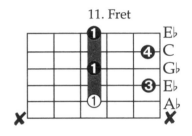

(no 5)

6. Fret

4. Fret

6. Fret

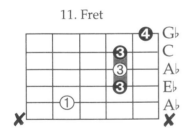

(3 in bass)

(no 5)

10. Fret

11. Fret

11. Fret

11. Fret

A♭9

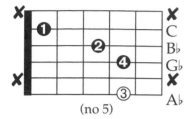

(no 5)

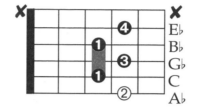

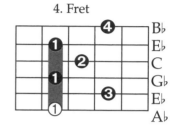

4. Fret

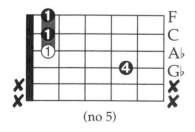

6. Fret

(no 5)

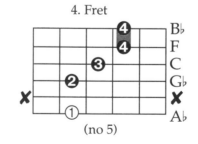

11. Fret

A♭
G♯

A♭13

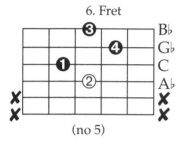

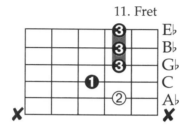

4. Fret

(no 5)

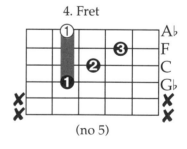

4. Fret

(no 5)

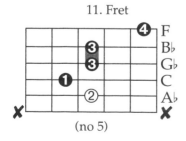

11. Fret

(no 5)

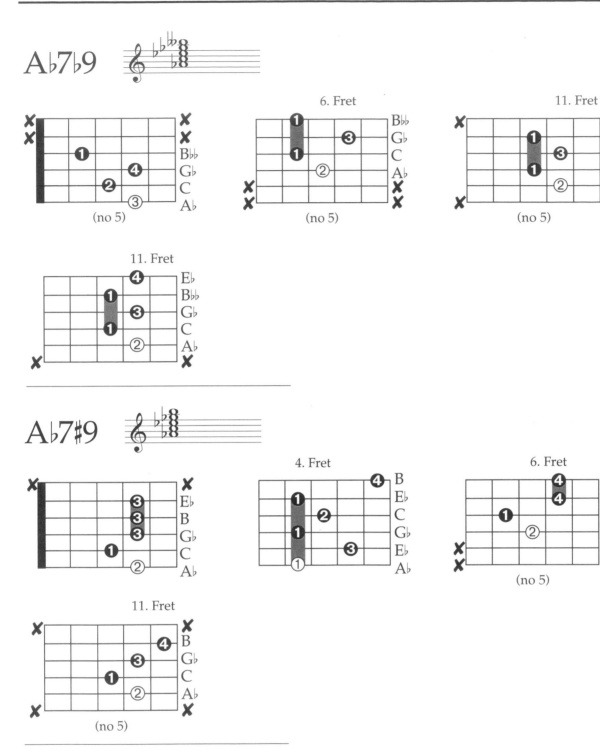

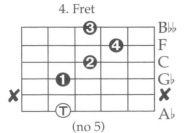

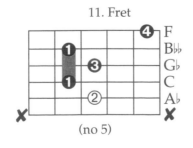

A♭7+

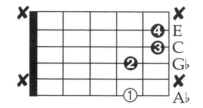

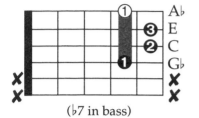

(♭7 in bass)

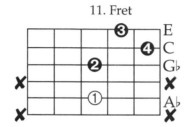

11. Fret

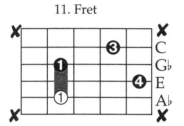

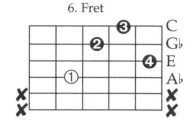

6. Fret

A♭7♭5

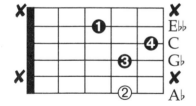

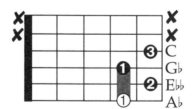

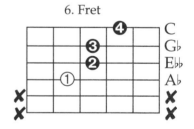

6. Fret

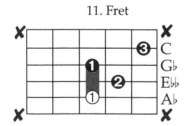

11. Fret

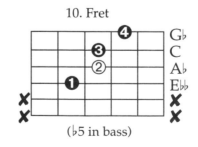

10. Fret

(♭5 in bass)

A♭7 ♭9 ♯5

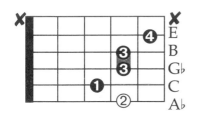

A♭7 ♯9 ♯5

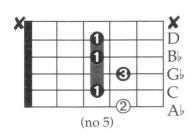

A♭9♯11

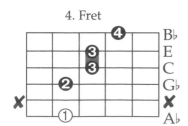

A♭9+

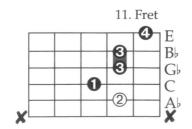

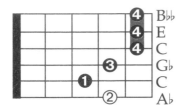

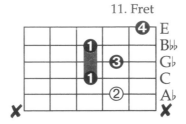

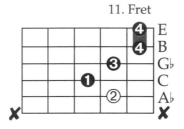

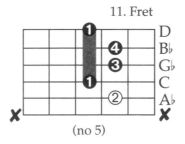

A♭
G♯

A♭7sus4

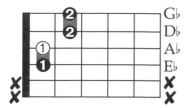

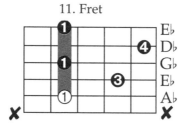

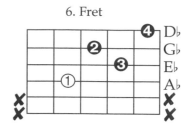

A♭9sus4

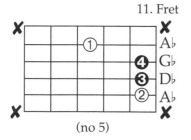

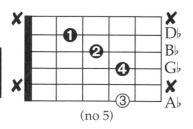

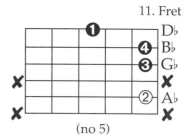

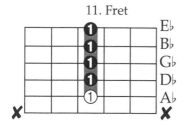

A♭13sus4

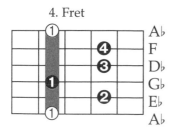

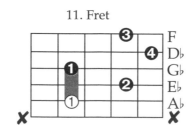

A♭°

4. Fret

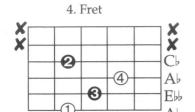

9. Fret

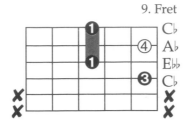

C♭
A♭
E♭♭
C♭

11. Fret

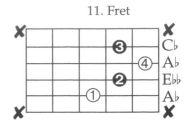

C♭
A♭
E♭♭
A♭

A♭m7♭5

4. Fret

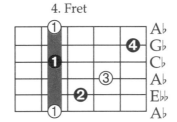

A♭
G♭
C♭
A♭
E♭♭
A♭

6. Fret

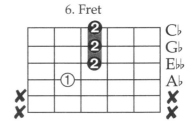

C♭
G♭
E♭♭
A♭

A♭
G♯

11. Fret

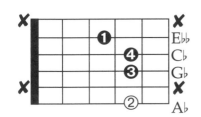

E♭♭
C♭
G♭
A♭

11. Fret

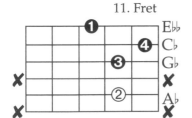

C♭
G♭
E♭♭
A♭

A♭°7

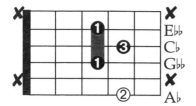

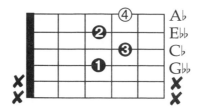

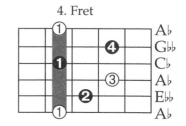

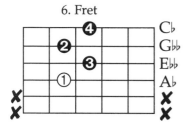

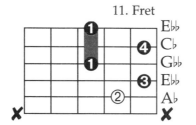

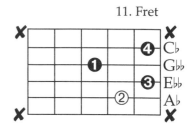

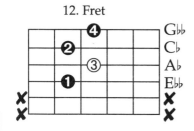

A♭
G♯

Ab+

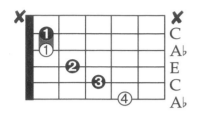
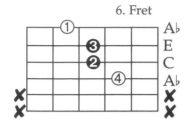
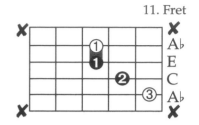

Absus4

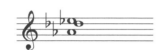

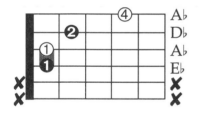
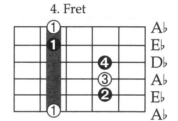
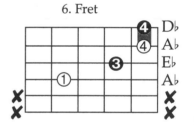

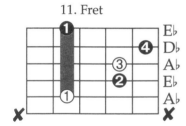

Absus2

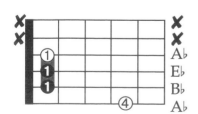
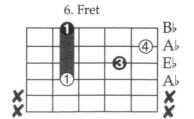
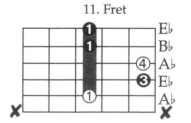

Ab
G#

A

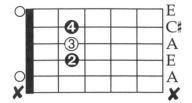

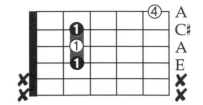

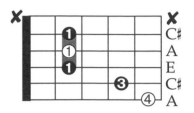

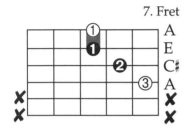

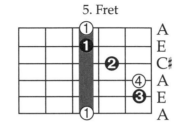

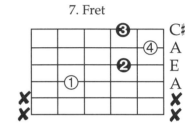

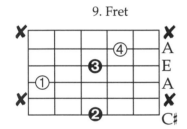

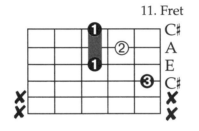

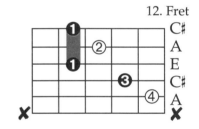

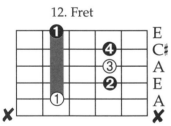

A6

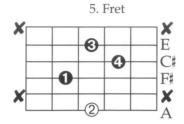

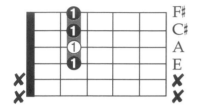

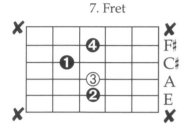

5. Fret
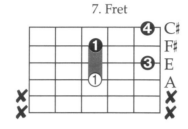

7. Fret
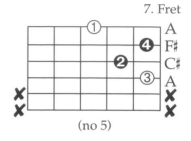
(no 5)

7. Fret
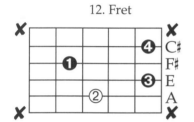

7. Fret
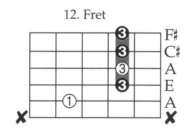

12. Fret
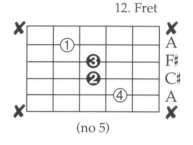
(no 5)

12. Fret
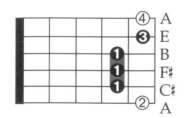

12. Fret
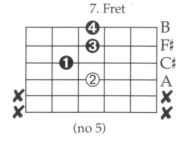

A

A 6/9

7. Fret
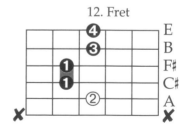
(no 5)

12. Fret

12. Fret
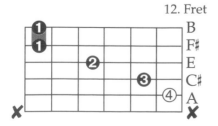

Amaj7

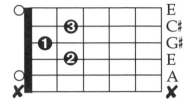
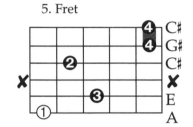
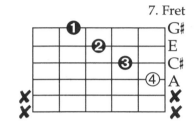

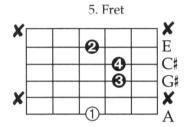
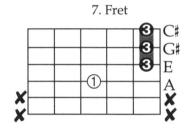
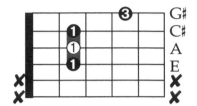

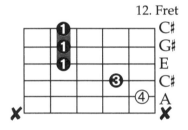

A

Amaj13

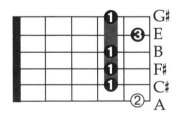
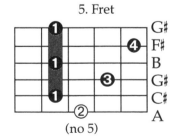
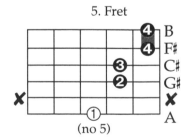

Amaj9

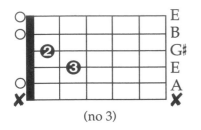
(no 3)

5. Fret

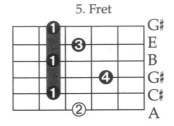

5. Fret

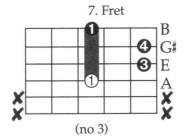

7. Fret

(no 5)

7. Fret

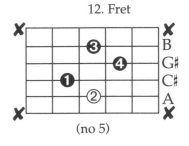
(no 3)

12. Fret

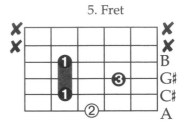
(no 5)

A

Amaj9#11

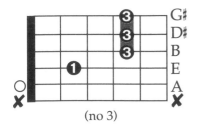
(no 3)

5. Fret

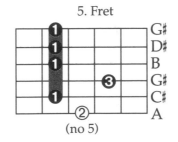
(no 5)

12. Fret

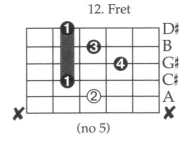
(no 5)

Amaj7+

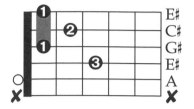

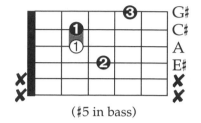

(♯5 in bass)

5. Fret

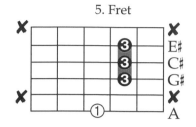

7. Fret

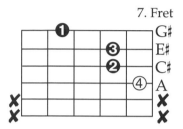

12. Fret

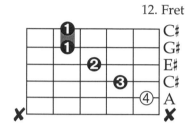

12. Fret

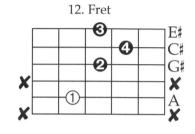

A

Amaj7♭5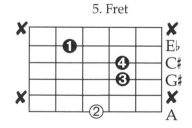

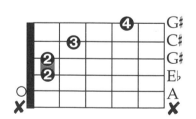

5. Fret

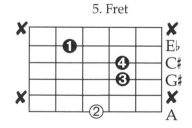

7. Fret

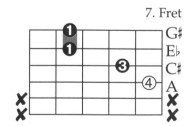

7. Fret

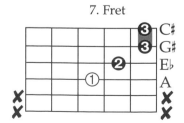

Amaj13(no9)

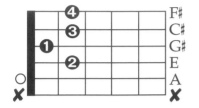

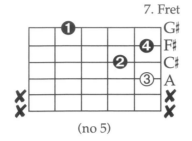

(no 5)

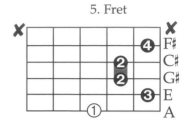

(no 5)

Aadd9

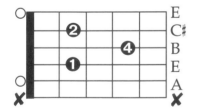

A

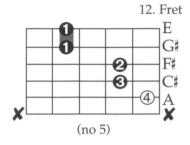

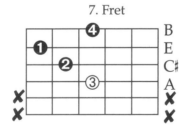

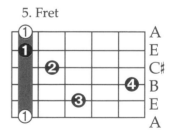

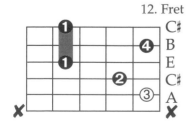

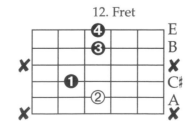

Am

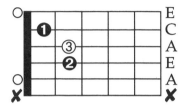

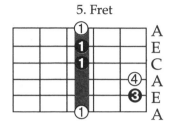
5. Fret

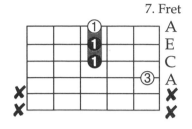
7. Fret

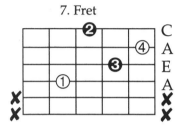
7. Fret

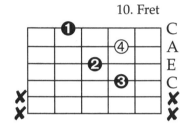
10. Fret

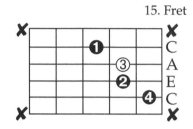
15. Fret

A Am7

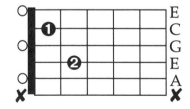

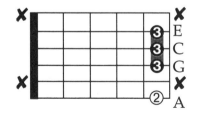

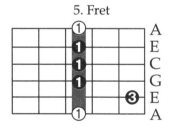
5. Fret

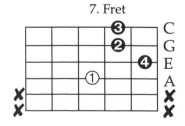
7. Fret

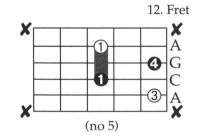
12. Fret
(no 5)

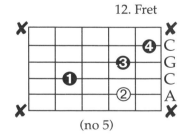
12. Fret
(no 5)

Am6

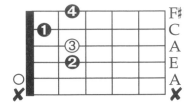

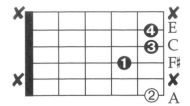

5. Fret

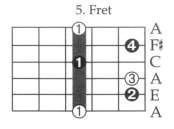

7. Fret

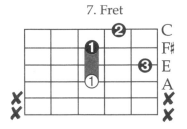

12. Fret

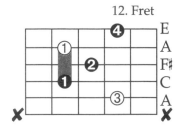

Am(maj7)

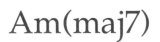

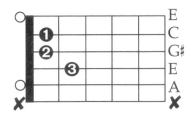

5. Fret

7. Fret

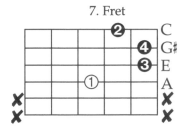

A

12. Fret

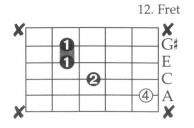

12. Fret

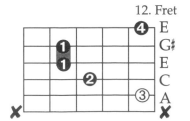

12. Fret

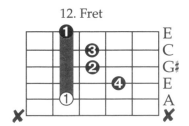

Am add9

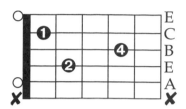

5. Fret

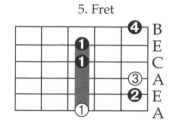

5. Fret

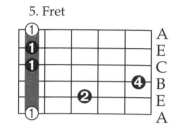

Am9

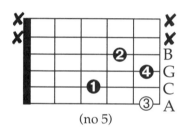

(no 5)

5. Fret

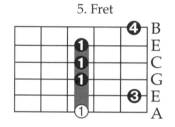

7. Fret

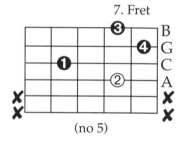

(no 5)

12. Fret

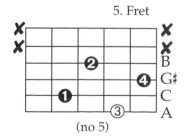

A

Am(maj9)

5. Fret

(no 5)

5. Fret

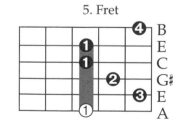

12. Fret

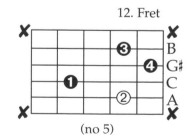

(no 5)

Am $\frac{6}{9}$

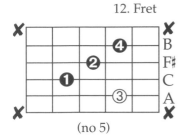

(no 5)

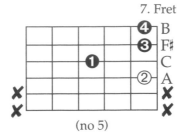

7. Fret

(no 5)

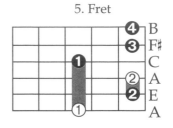

5. Fret

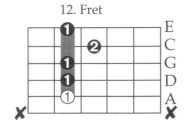

12. Fret

(no 5)

Am11(no9)

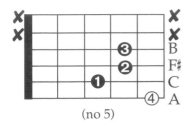

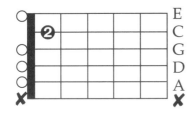

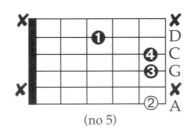

(no 5)

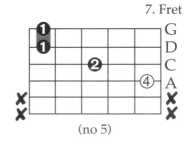

7. Fret

(no 5)

12. Fret

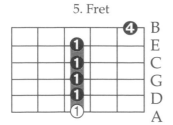

Am11

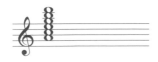

5. Fret

A

A7

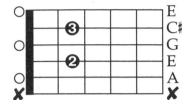
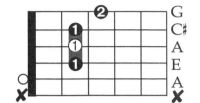
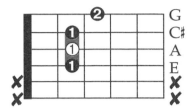

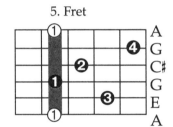
5. Fret
(♭7 in bass)

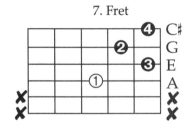
5. Fret

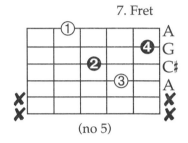
7. Fret
(no 5)

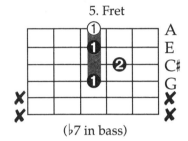
5. Fret

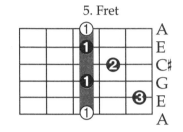
7. Fret

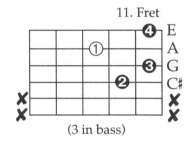
11. Fret
(3 in bass)

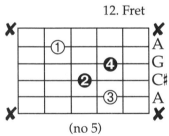
12. Fret
(no 5)

A9

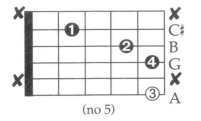

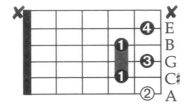

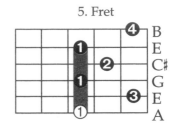

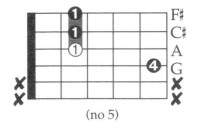

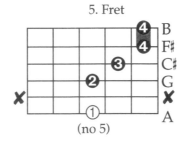

A13

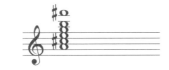

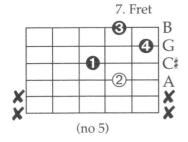

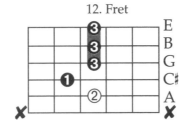

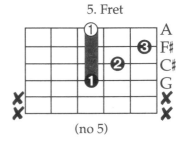

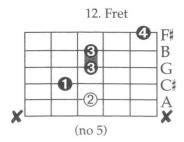

A

A7♭9

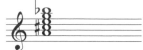

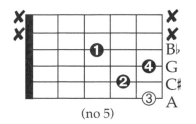
(no 5)

7. Fret
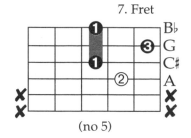
(no 5)

12. Fret
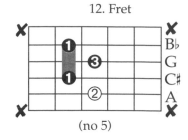
(no 5)

12. Fret
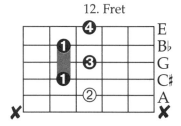

A7♯9

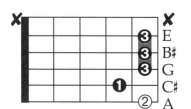

5. Fret
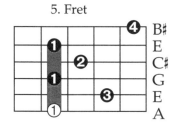

7. Fret
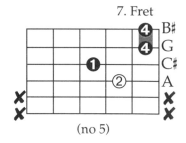
(no 5)

12. Fret
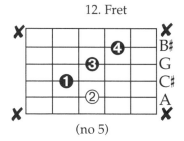
(no 5)

A13♭9

5. Fret
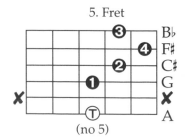
(no 5)

12. Fret
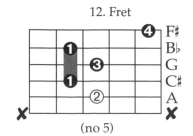
(no 5)

A7+

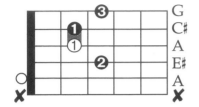

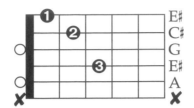

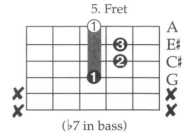

5. Fret

(♭7 in bass)

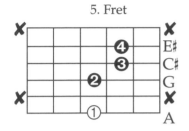

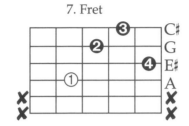

5. Fret

7. Fret

A7♭5

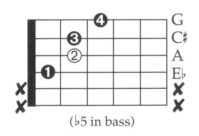

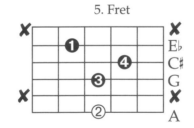

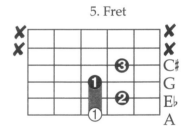

5. Fret

5. Fret

(♭5 in bass)

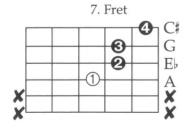

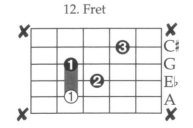

7. Fret

12. Fret

A

A7$^{\flat 9}_{\sharp 5}$

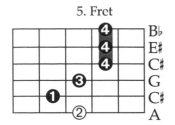

5. Fret | 12. Fret

A7$^{\sharp 9}_{\sharp 5}$

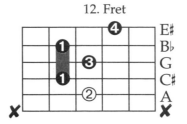

5. Fret | 12. Fret

A9$\sharp$11

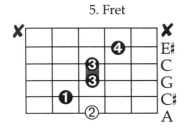

5. Fret | 12. Fret

(no 5)   (no 5)

A9+

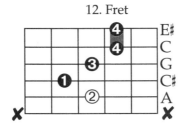

5. Fret | 12. Fret

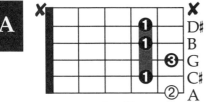

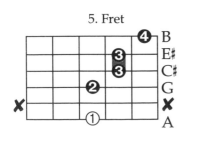

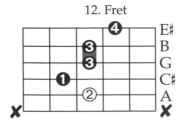

A7sus4

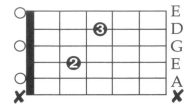
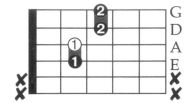
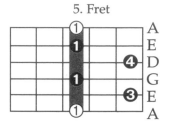

5. Fret

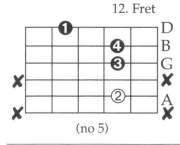
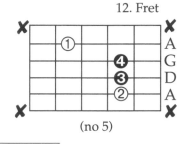

7. Fret   12. Fret

(no 5)

A9sus4

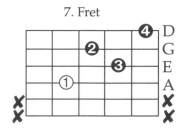

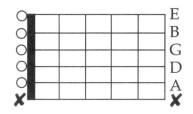
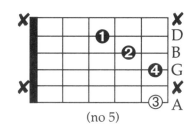
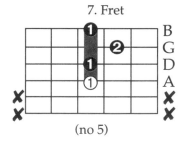

7. Fret

(no 5)   (no 5)

12. Fret

(no 5)

A

A13sus4

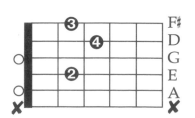
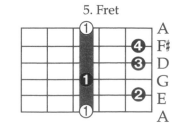

5. Fret

A°

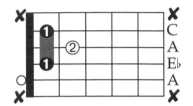

5. Fret

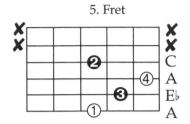

10. Fret

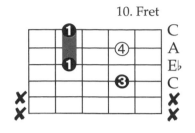

Am7♭5

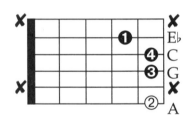

5. Fret

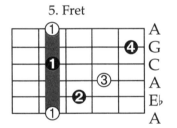

7. Fret

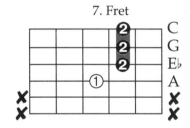

A

12. Fret

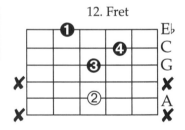

12. Fret

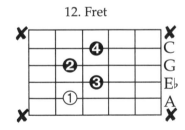

A°7

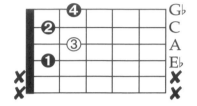

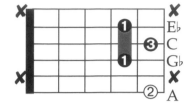

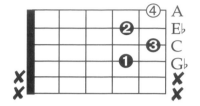

5. Fret

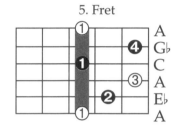

7. Fret

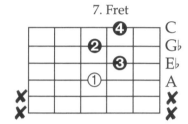

12. Fret

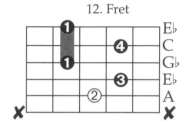

12. Fret

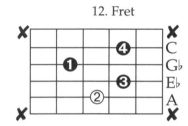

A

A+

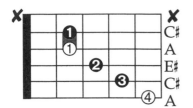
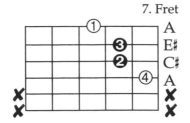
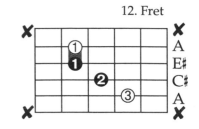

Asus4

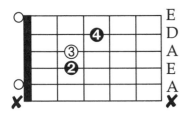
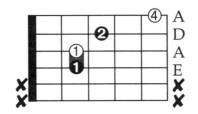
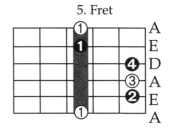

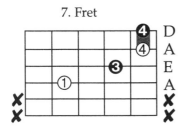

A

Asus2

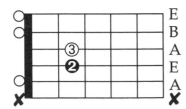
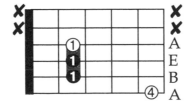
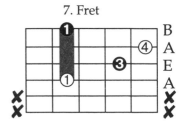

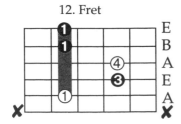

B♭

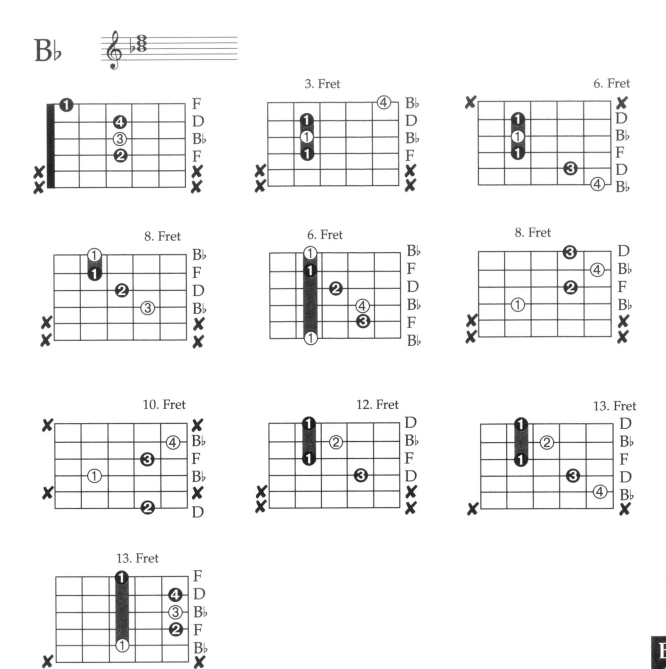

Bb6

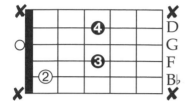

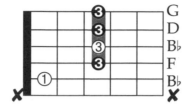

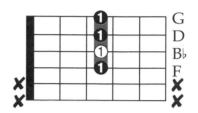

6. Fret

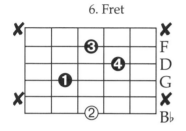

8. Fret

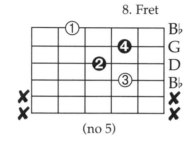

(no 5)

8. Fret

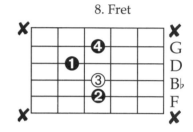

8. Fret

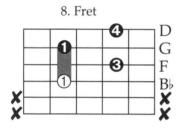

13. Fret

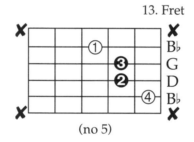

(no 5)

Bb 6/9

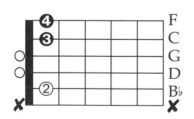

6. Fret

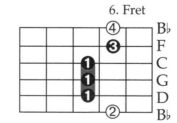

8. Fret

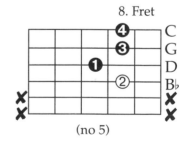

(no 5)

13. Fret

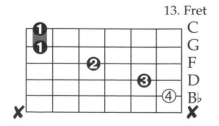

B♭maj7

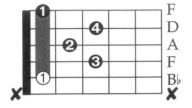   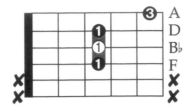   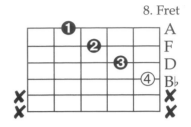

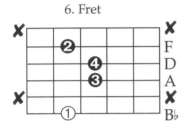   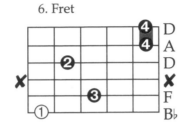   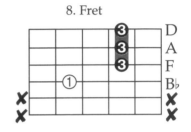

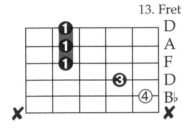

B♭maj13

Bb
A#

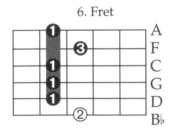   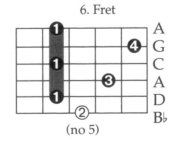   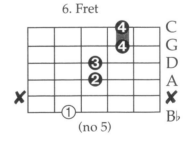

Bbmaj9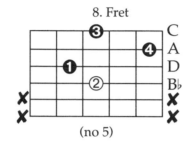

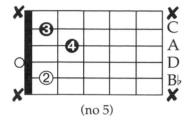
(no 5)

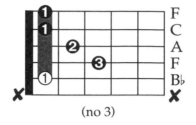
(no 3)

6. Fret
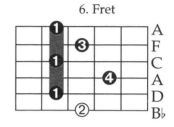

6. Fret
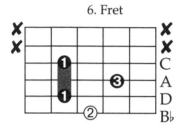

8. Fret
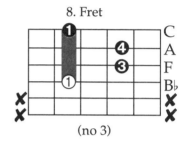
(no 5)

8. Fret
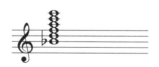
(no 3)

Bb
A#

Bbmaj9#11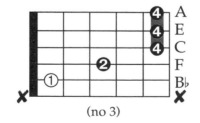

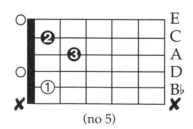
(no 5)

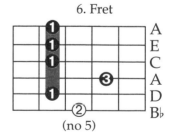
(no 3)

6. Fret
(no 5)

B♭maj7+

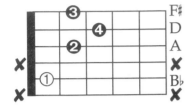

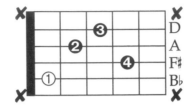

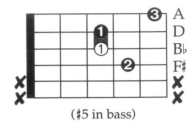

(♯5 in bass)

8. Fret

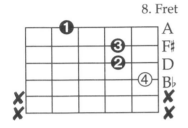

6. Fret

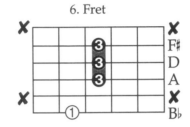

13. Fret

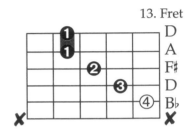

B♭maj7♭5

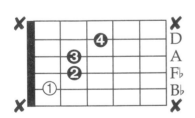

6. Fret

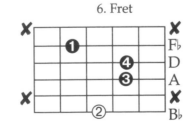

8. Fret

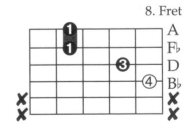

8. Fret

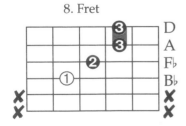

B♭
A♯

B♭maj13(no9)

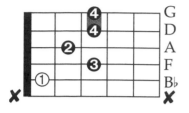

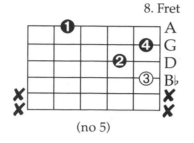

8. Fret

(no 5)

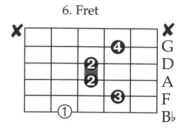

6. Fret

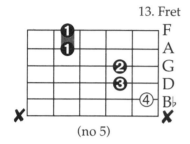

13. Fret

(no 5)

B♭add9

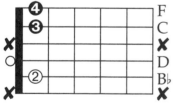

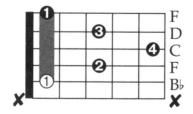

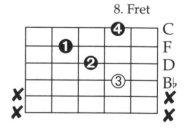

8. Fret

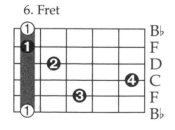

6. Fret

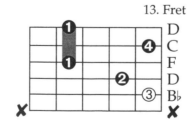

13. Fret

B♭m

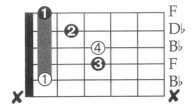

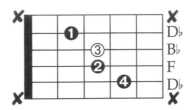

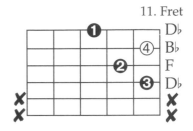

6. Fret

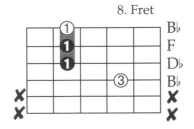

8. Fret

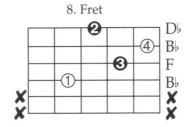

8. Fret

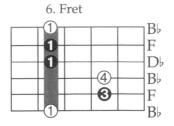

11. Fret

B♭m7

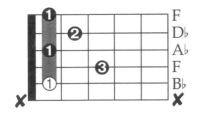

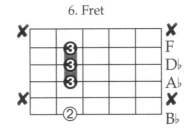

6. Fret

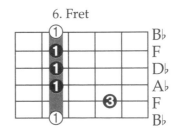

6. Fret

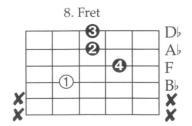

8. Fret

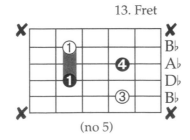

13. Fret

(no 5)

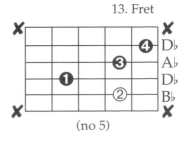

13. Fret

(no 5)

B♭
A♯

B♭m6

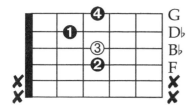
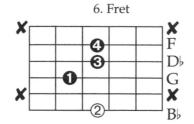
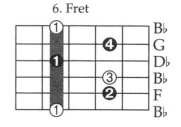

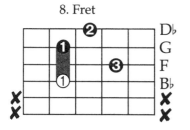
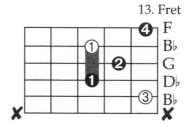

B♭m(maj7)

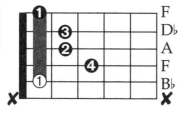
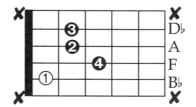
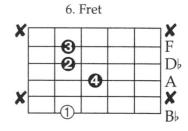

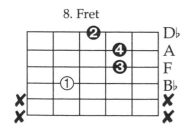
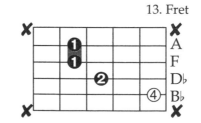
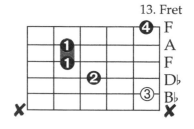

B♭m add9

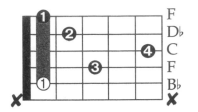

B♭m9

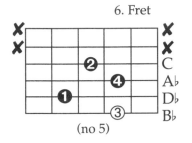

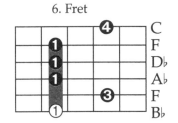

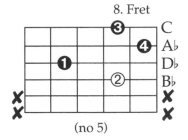

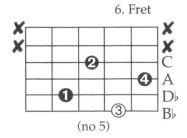

B♭
A♯

B♭m(maj9)

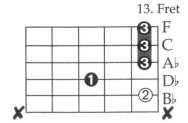

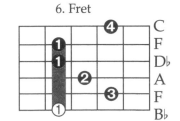

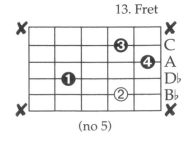

B♭m $\frac{6}{9}$

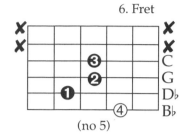

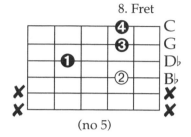

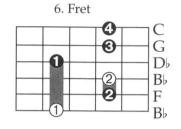

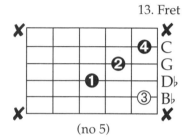

B♭m11(no9)

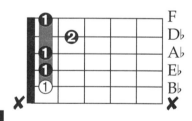

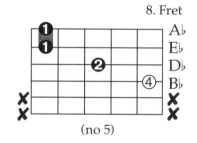

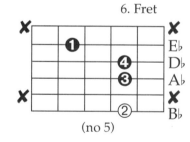

B♭m11

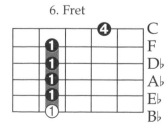

B♭7

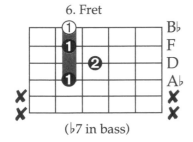

F
D
A♭
F
B♭

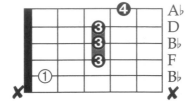

A♭
D
B♭
F
B♭

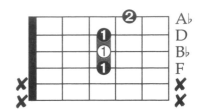

A♭
D
B♭
F

6. Fret

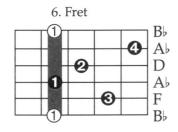

B♭
F
D
A♭

(♭7 in bass)

6. Fret

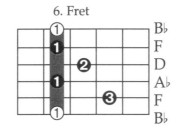

B♭
F
D
A♭
F
B♭

8. Fret

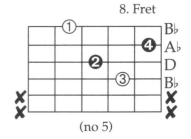

B♭
A♭
D
B♭

(no 5)

6. Fret

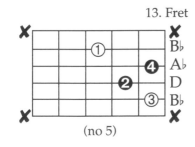

B♭
A♭
D
A♭
F
B♭

8. Fret

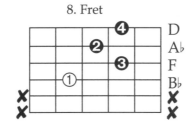

D
A♭
F
B♭

12. Fret

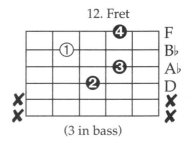

F
B♭
A♭
D

(3 in bass)

13. Fret

B♭
A♭
D
B♭

(no 5)

B♭
A♯

B♭9

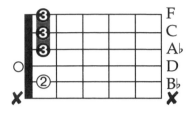

F
C
A♭
D
B♭

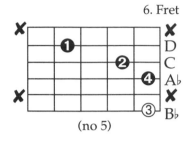

6. Fret

D
C
A♭

B♭

(no 5)

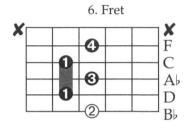

6. Fret

F
C
A♭
D
B♭

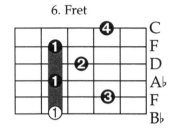

6. Fret

C
F
D
A♭
F
B♭

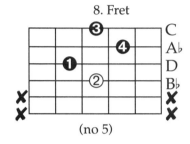

8. Fret

C
A♭
D
B♭

(no 5)

B♭13

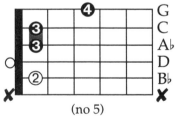

(no 5)

G
C
A♭
D
B♭

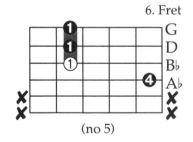

6. Fret

G
D
B♭
A♭

(no 5)

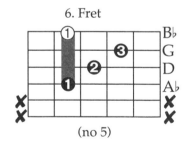

6. Fret

B♭
G
D
A♭

(no 5)

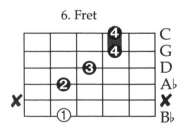

6. Fret

C
G
D
A♭
B♭

B♭7♭9

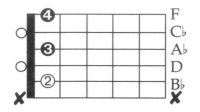

F
C♭
A♭
D
B♭

6. Fret

C♭
A♭
D
B♭
(no 5)

8. Fret

C♭
A♭
D♭
B♭
(no 5)

13. Fret

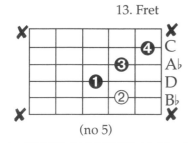

C♭
A♭
D
B♭
(no 5)

B♭7♯9

6. Fret

F
C♯
A♭
D
B♭

6. Fret

C♯
F
D
A♭
F
B♭

8. Fret

C♯
A♭
D
B♭
(no 5)

13. Fret

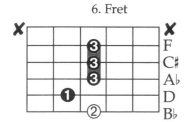

C
A♭
D
B♭
(no 5)

B♭13♭9

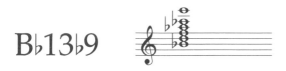

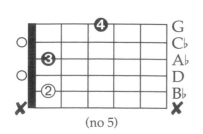

G
C♭
A♭
D
B♭
(no 5)

6. Fret

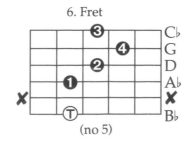

C♭
G
D
A♭
B♭
(no 5)

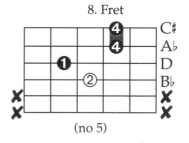

B♭
A♯

B♭7+

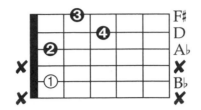
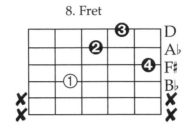
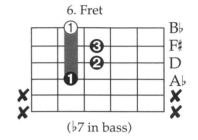

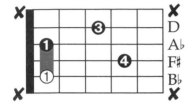
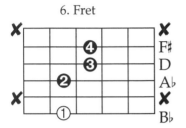

B♭7♭5

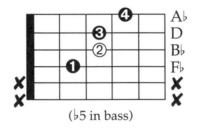
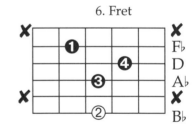

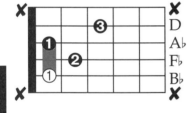
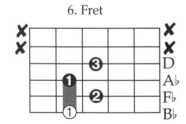
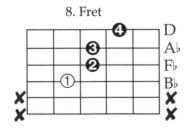

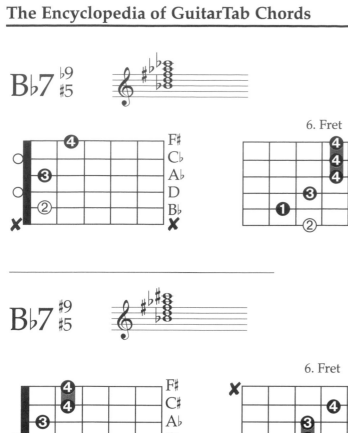

B♭7 ♭9/#5

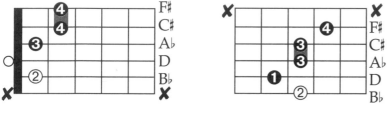

B♭7 #9/#5

B♭9#11

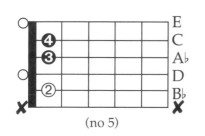
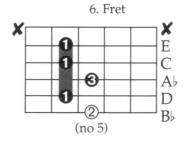

B♭9+

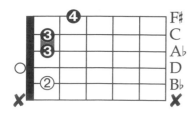
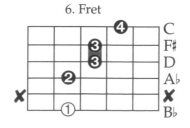

B♭
A#

B♭7sus4

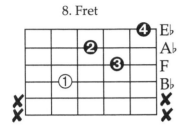

8. Fret

B♭9sus4

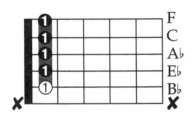

13. Fret

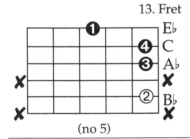

(no 5)

B♭13sus4

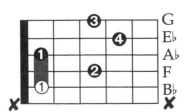

Bb°

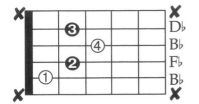

6. Fret

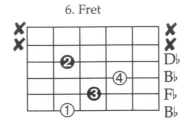

11. Fret

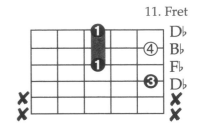

Bbm7b5

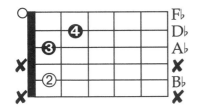

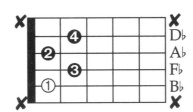

6. Fret

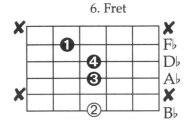

6. Fret

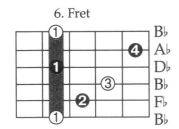

8. Fret

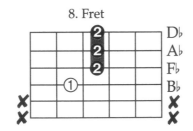

B♭°7

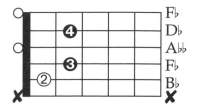

F♭
D♭
A♭♭
F♭
B♭

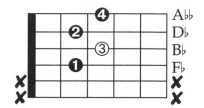

A♭♭
D♭
B♭
F♭

6. Fret

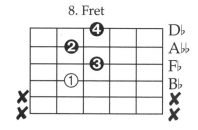

F♭
D♭
A♭♭

B♭

5. Fret

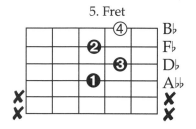

B♭
F♭
D♭
A♭♭

6. Fret

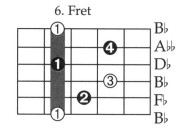

B♭
A♭♭
D♭
B♭
F♭
B♭

8. Fret

D♭
A♭♭
F♭
B♭

13. Fret

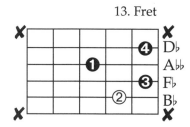

D♭
A♭♭
F♭
B♭

B♭
A♯

Bb+

6. Fret

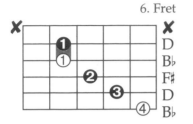

D
Bb
F#
D
Bb

8. Fret

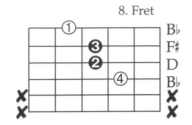

Bb
F#
D
Bb

13. Fret

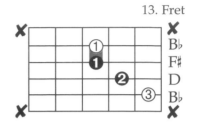

Bb
F#
D
Bb

Bbsus4

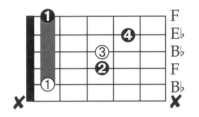

F
Eb
Bb
F
Bb

6. Fret

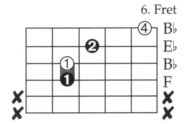

Bb
Eb
Bb
F

6. Fret

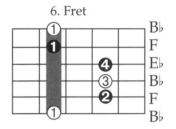

Bb
F
Eb
Bb
F
Bb

8. Fret

Eb
Bb
F
Bb

Bbsus2

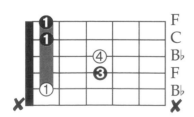

F
C
Bb
F
Bb

6. Fret

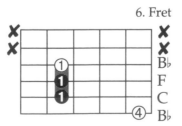

Bb
F
C
Bb

8. Fret

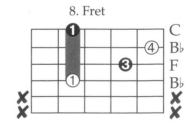

C
Bb
F
Bb

Bb
A#

B

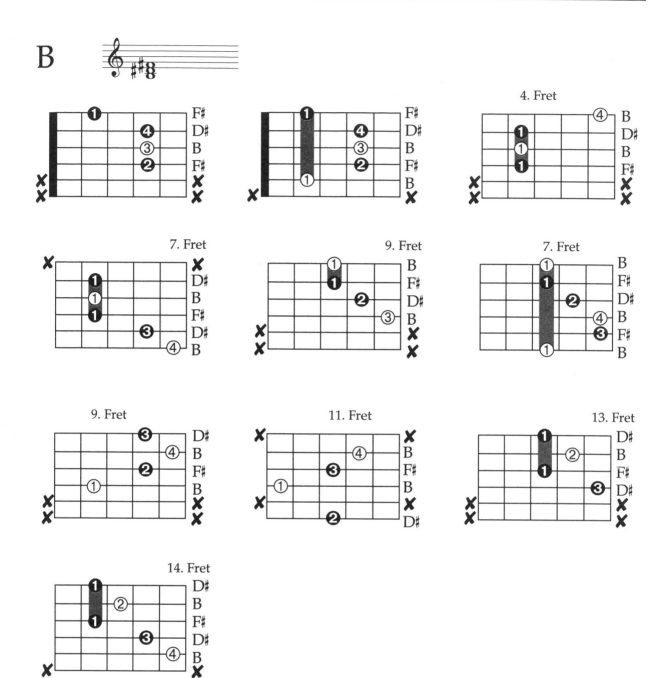

B6

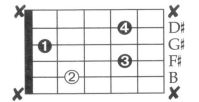
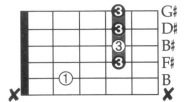
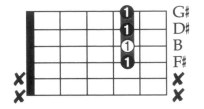

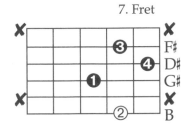

7. Fret

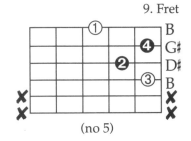

9. Fret

(no 5)

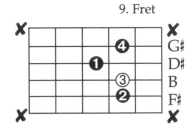

9. Fret

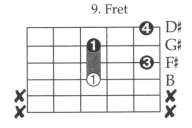

9. Fret

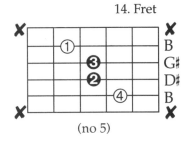

14. Fret

(no 5)

B$^6_9$

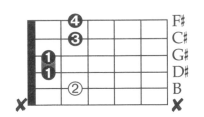

7. Fret

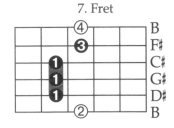

9. Fret

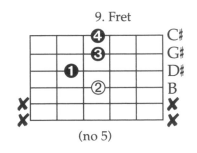

(no 5)

14. Fret

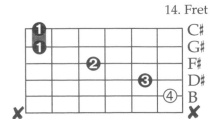

B

Bmaj7

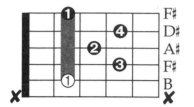

4. Fret
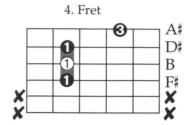

9. Fret
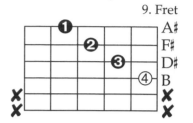

7. Fret
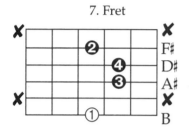

7. Fret
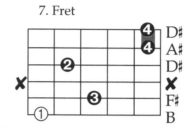

9. Fret
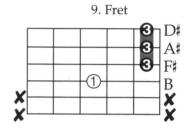

14. Fret
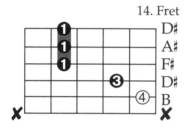

Bmaj13

7. Fret
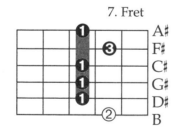

7. Fret
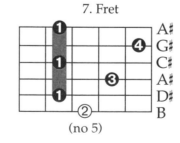
(no 5)

7. Fret
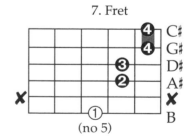
(no 5)

Bmaj9

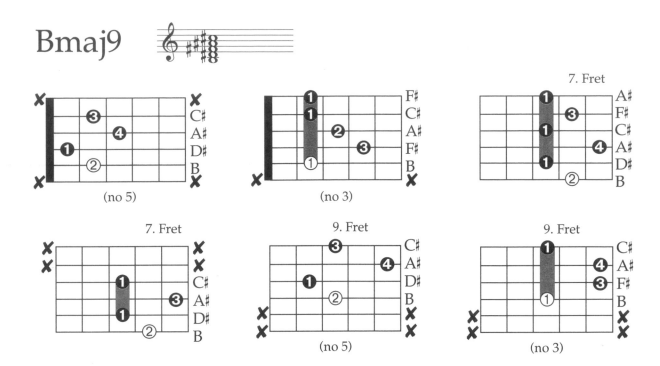

Bmaj9#11

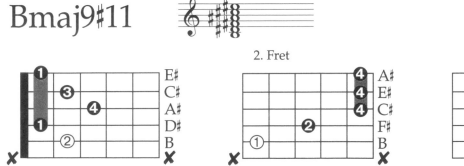

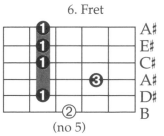

Bmaj7+

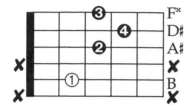
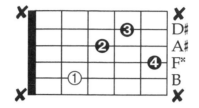
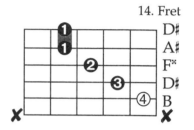

(♯5 in bass)

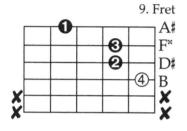
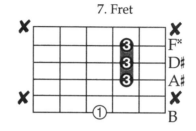
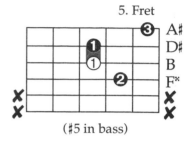

Bmaj7♭5

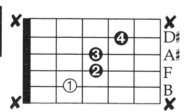
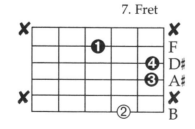
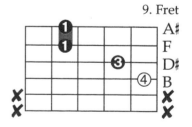

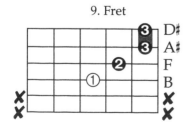

Bmaj13(no9)

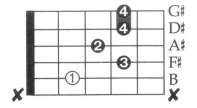

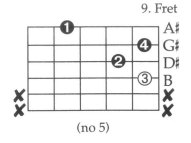

(no 5)

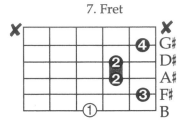

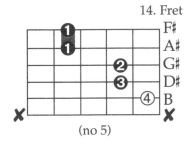

(no 5)

Badd9

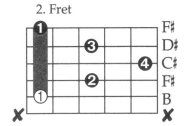

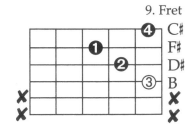

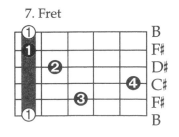

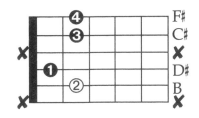

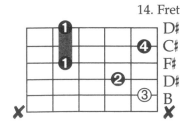

B

Bm

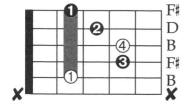
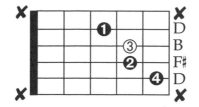
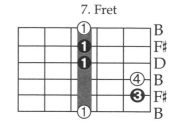

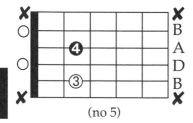
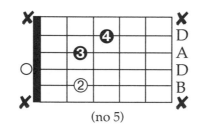
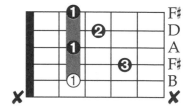

Bm7

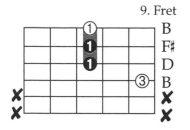
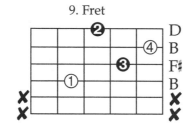
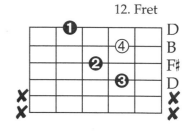

(no 5)   (no 5)

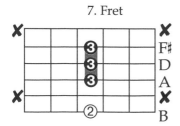
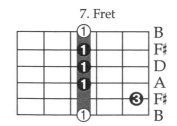
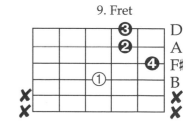

Bm6

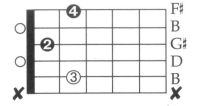

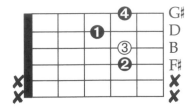

7. Fret

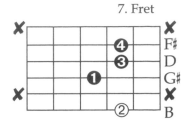

7. Fret

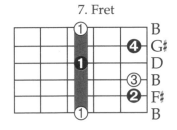

9. Fret

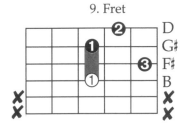

Bm(maj7)

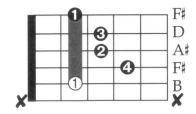

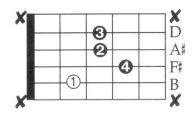

7. Fret

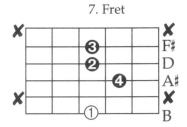

9. Fret

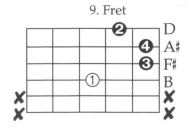

14. Fret

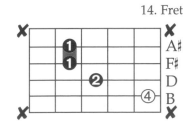

14. Fret

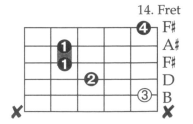

B

Bm add9

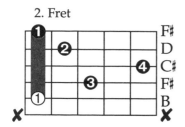

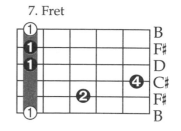

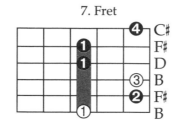

Bm9

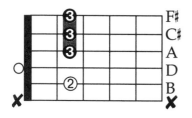

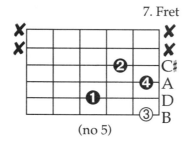

(no 5)

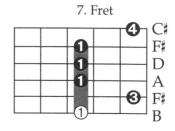

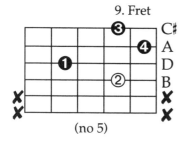

(no 5)

B Bm(maj9)

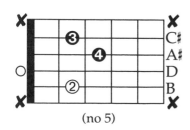

(no 5)

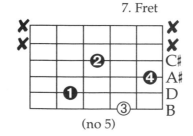

(no 5)

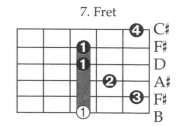

Bm $^6_9$

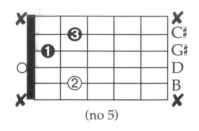
(no 5)

7. Fret
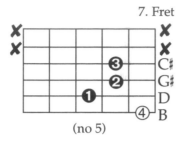
(no 5)

9. Fret
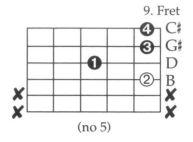
(no 5)

7. Fret
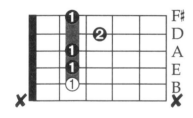

Bm11(no9)

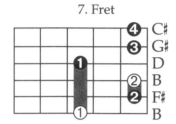

9. Fret
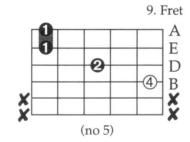
(no 5)

7. Fret
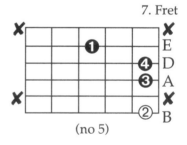
(no 5)

Bm11

7. Fret
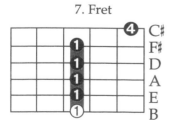

B

B7

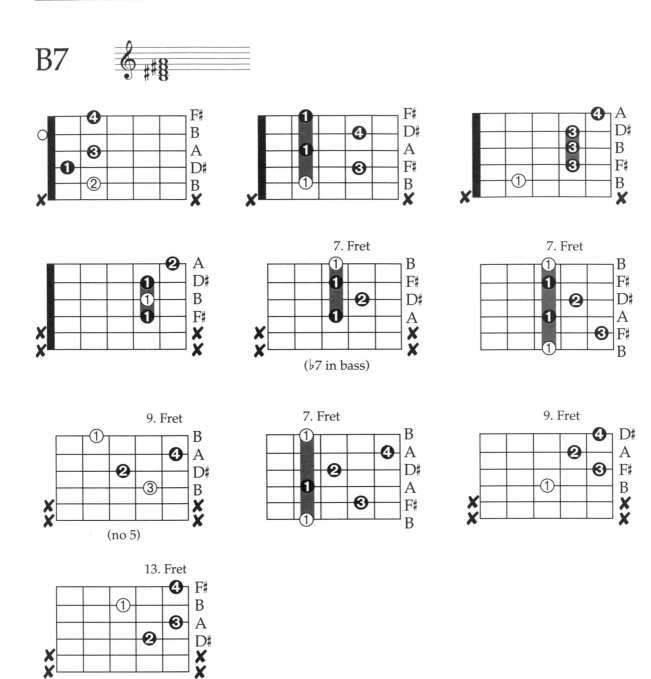

B9

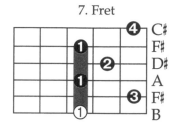

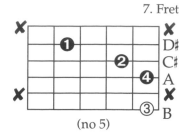

7. Fret

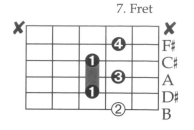

7. Fret

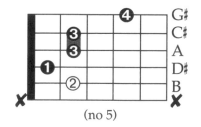

7. Fret

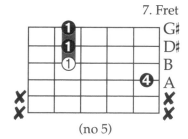

9. Fret

B13

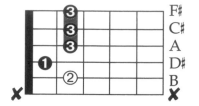

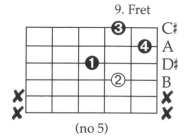

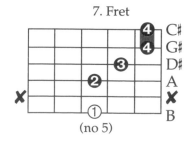

7. Fret

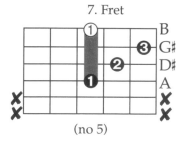

7. Fret

B

B7♭9

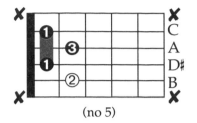

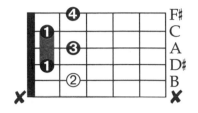

7. Fret

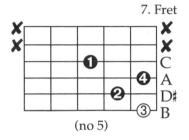

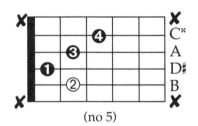

9. Fret

B7♯9
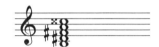

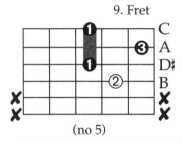

7. Fret

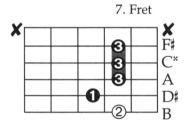

7. Fret

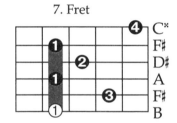

9. Fret

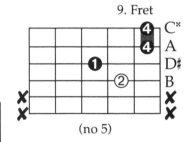

B13♭9

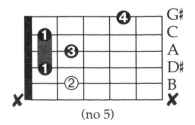

7. Fret

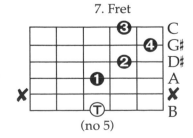

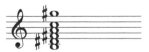

B

B7+

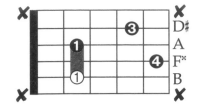

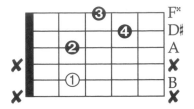

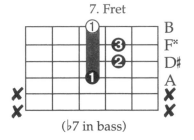

(♭7 in bass)

7. Fret

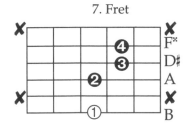

9. Fret

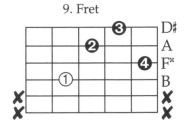

B7♭5

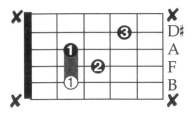

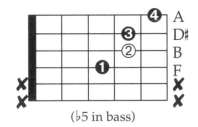

7. Fret

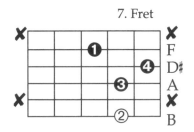

(♭5 in bass)

7. Fret

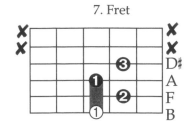

9. Fret

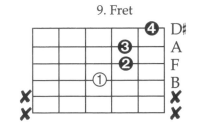

B

B7 $^{\flat 9}_{\sharp 5}$

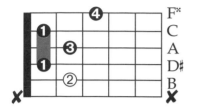

B7 $^{\sharp 9}_{\sharp 5}$

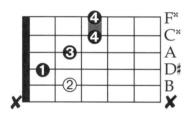

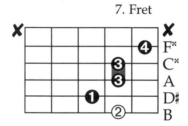

B9$\sharp$11

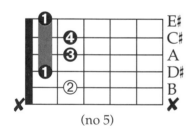

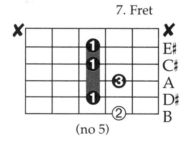

(no 5)   (no 5)

B9+

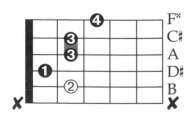

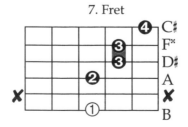

B7sus4

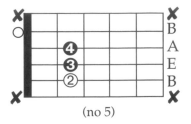 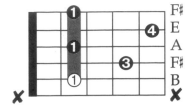 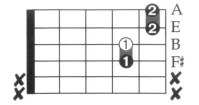

(no 5)

7. Fret

9. Fret

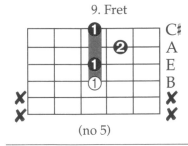 

B9sus4

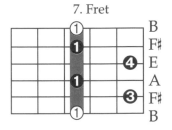 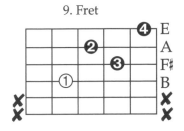 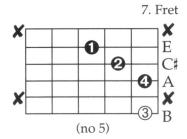

(no 5)

7. Fret

(no 5)

9. Fret

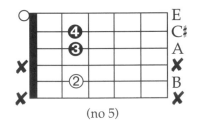 

(no 5)

B13sus4

7. Fret

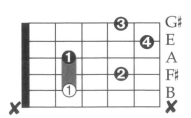 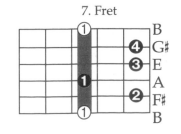 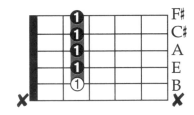

B

B°

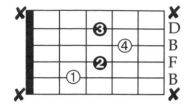

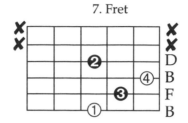

7. Fret

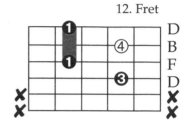

12. Fret

Bm7♭5

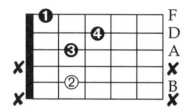

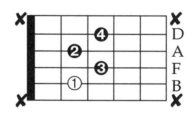

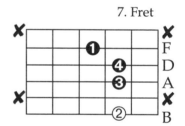

7. Fret

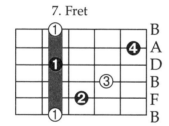

7. Fret

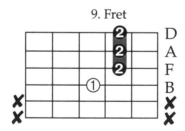

9. Fret

B

B°7

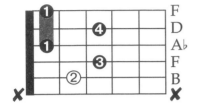

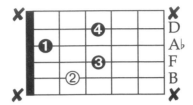

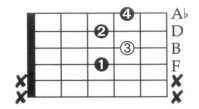

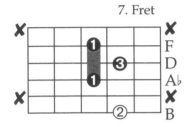

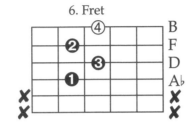

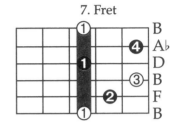

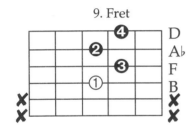

B+

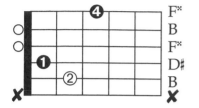   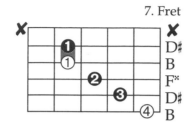   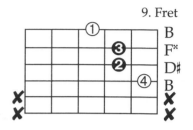

Bsus4

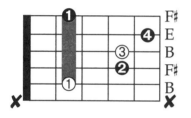   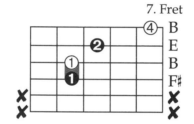   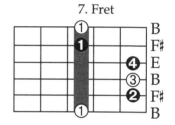

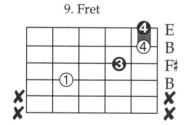

B

Bsus2

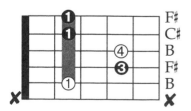   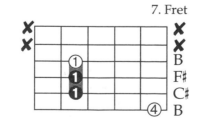   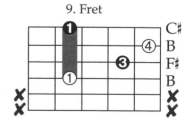

E5 (E/Em)

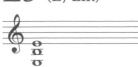
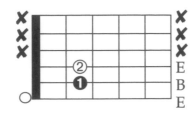

F5 (F/Fm)

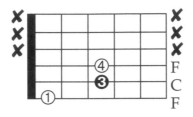

F♯5 (F♯/F♯m)

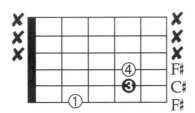

G5 (G/Gm)

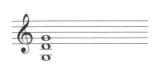
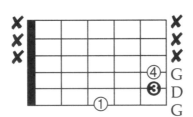

A♭5 (A♭/A♭m)

4. Fret

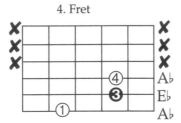

A5 (A/Am)

5. Fret

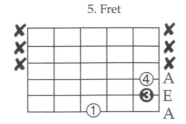

B♭5 (B♭/B♭m)

6. Fret

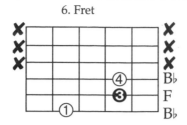

B♭
F
B♭

B5 (B/Bm)

7. Fret

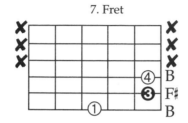

B
F#
B

C5 (C/Cm)

8. Fret

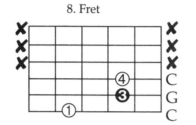

C
G
C

C♯5 (C♯/C♯m)

9. Fret

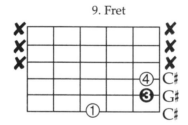

C#
G#
C#

D5 (D/Dm)

10. Fret

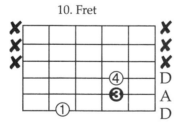

D
A
D

E♭5 (E♭/E♭m)

11. Fret

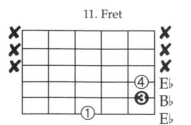

E♭
B♭
E♭

A5 (A/Am)

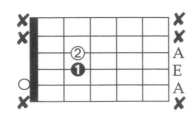

Bb5 (Bb/Bbm)

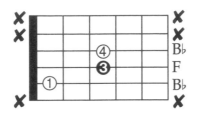

B5 (B/Bm)

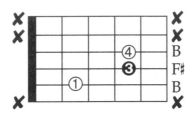

C5 (C/Cm)

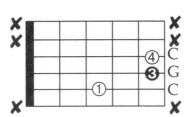

C#5 (C#/C#m)

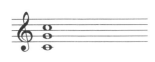

4. Fret

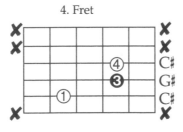

D5 (D/Dm)

5. Fret

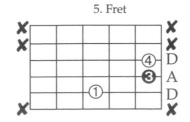

POWER CHORDS

6. Fret

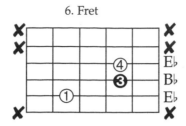

E5 (E/Em)

7. Fret

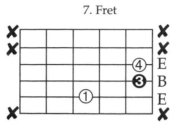

F5 (F/Fm)

8. Fret

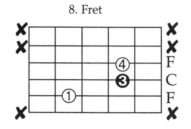

F#5 (F#/F#m)

9. Fret

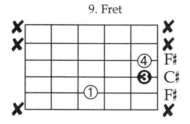

G5 (G/Gm)

10. Fret

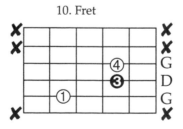

Ab5 (Ab/Abm)

11. Fret

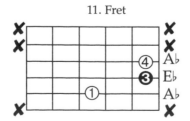

D5 (D/Dm)

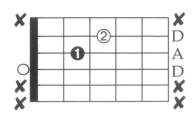

E♭5 (E♭/E♭m)

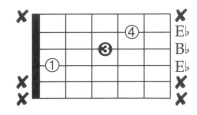

E5 (E/Em)

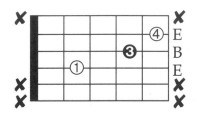

F5 (F/Fm)

3. Fret

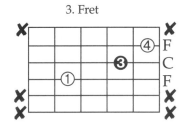

F♯5 (F♯/F♯m)

4. Fret

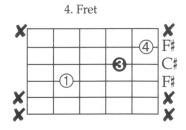

G5 (G/Gm)

5. Fret

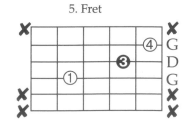

A♭5 (A♭/A♭m)

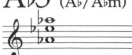
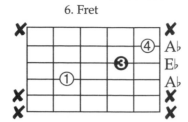

A5 (A/Am)

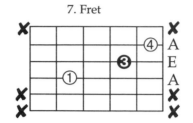

B♭5 (B♭/B♭m)

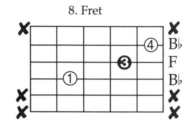

B5 (B/Bm)

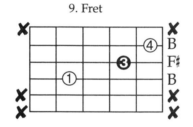

C5 (C/Cm)

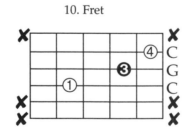

C♯5 (C♯/C♯m)

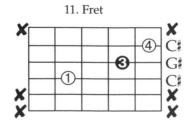

POWER CHORDS

Esus4

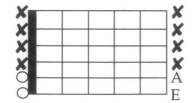

Fsus4

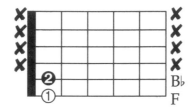

F#sus4

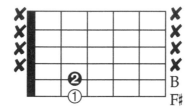

Gsus4

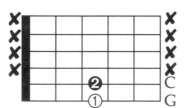

Absus4

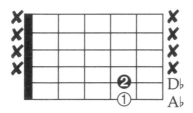

Asus4

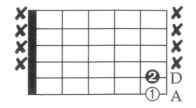

POWER CHORDS

B♭sus4

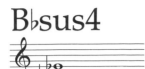
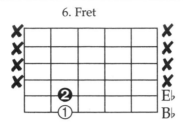

6. Fret

E♭
B♭

Bsus4

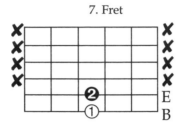

7. Fret

E
B

Csus4

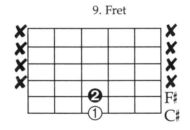

8. Fret

F
C

C♯sus4

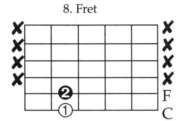

9. Fret

F♯
C♯

Dsus4

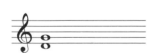
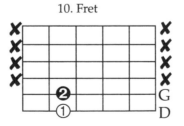

10. Fret

G
D

E♭sus4

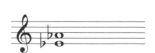
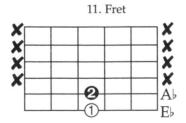

11. Fret

A♭
E♭

POWER CHORDS

Asus4

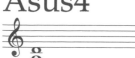
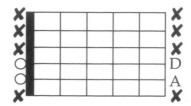

B♭sus4

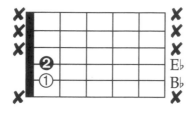

Bsus4

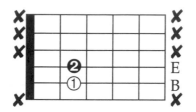

Csus4

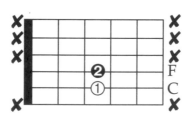

C♯sus4

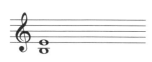
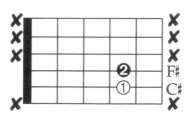

Dsus4

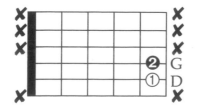

POWER CHORDS

E♭sus4

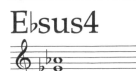

6. Fret

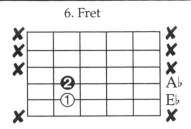

A♭
E♭

Esus4

7. Fret

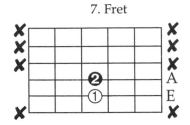

A
E

Fsus4

8. Fret

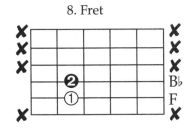

B♭
F

F♯sus4

9. Fret

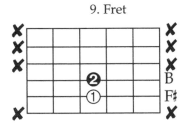

B
F♯

Gsus4

10. Fret

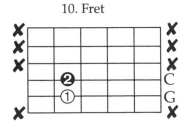

C
G

POWER CHORDS

A♭sus4

11. Fret

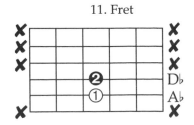

D♭
A♭

Dsus4

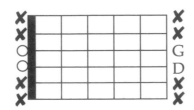

Ebsus4

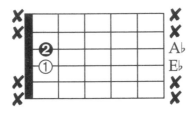

Esus4

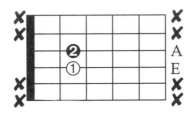

Fsus4

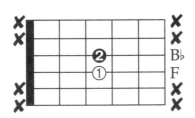

F#sus4

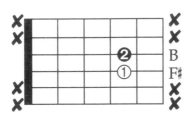

Gsus4

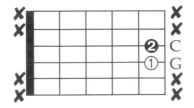

A♭sus4

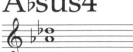
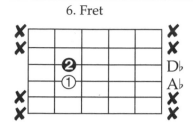

6. Fret

D♭
A♭

Asus4

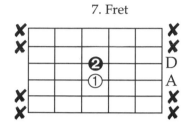

7. Fret

D
A

B♭sus4

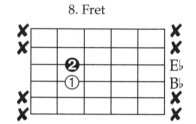

8. Fret

E♭
B♭

Bsus4

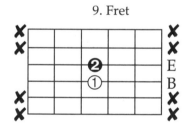

9. Fret

E
B

Csus4

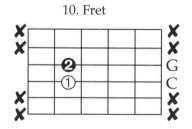

10. Fret

G
C

C♯sus4

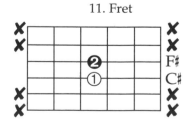

11. Fret

F♯
C♯

E5°

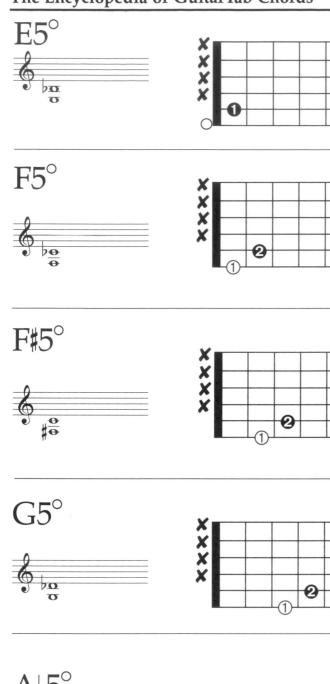

F5°

F#5°

G5°

Ab5°

A5°

5. Fret

B♭5°

6. Fret

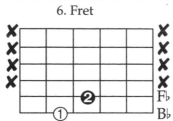

B5°

7. Fret

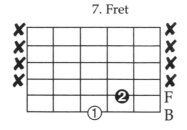

C5°

8. Fret

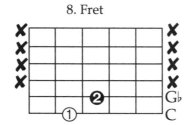

C♯5°

9. Fret

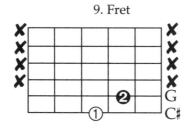

D5°

10. Fret

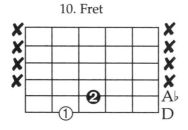

E♭5°

11. Fret

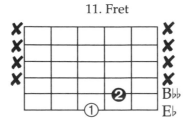

A5°

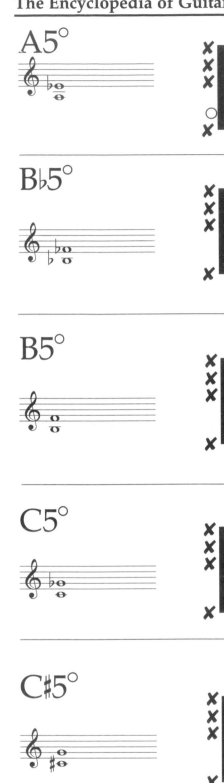

Bb5°

B5°

C5°

C#5°

D5°

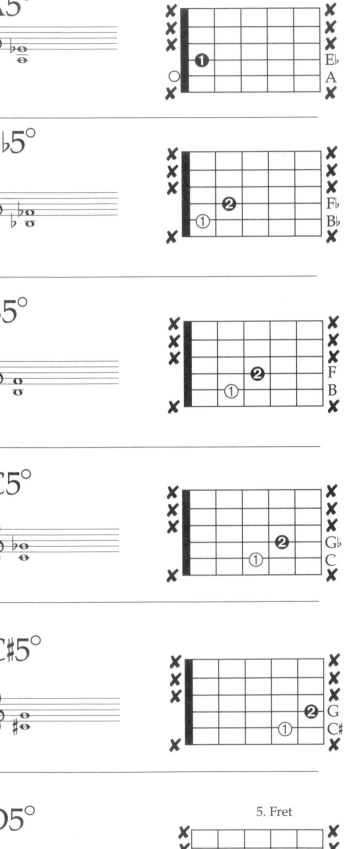

5. Fret

E♭5°

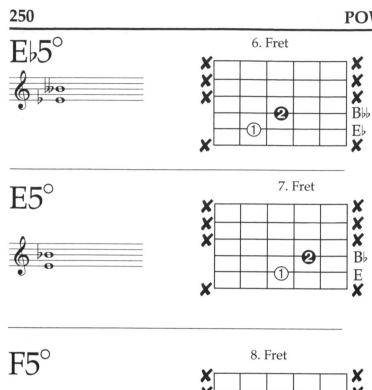

6. Fret

E5°

7. Fret

F5°

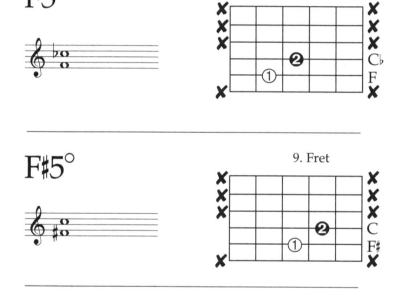

8. Fret

F♯5°

9. Fret

G5°

10. Fret

A♭5°

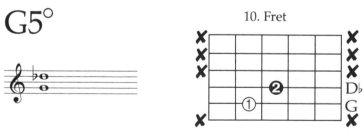

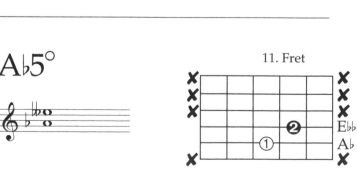

11. Fret

D5°

E♭5°

E5°

F5°

F♯5°

G5°

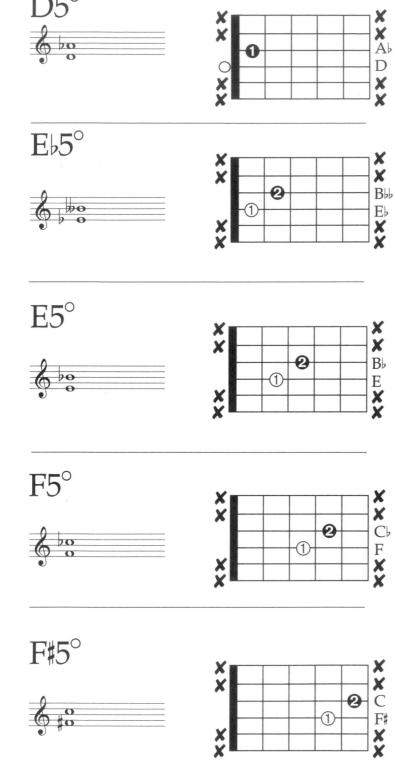

5. Fret

POWER CHORDS

A♭5°

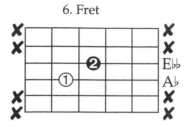

6. Fret

A5°

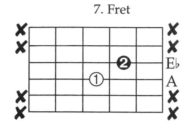

7. Fret

B♭5°

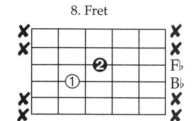

8. Fret

B5°

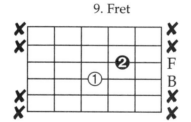

9. Fret

C5°

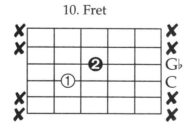

10. Fret

C♯5°

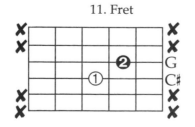

11. Fret

C3

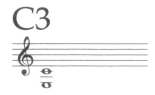

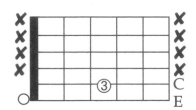

C#3

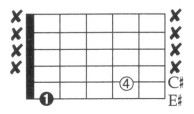

D3

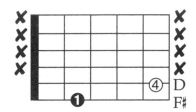

Eb3

3. Fret

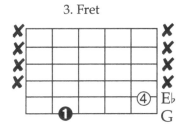

E3

4. Fret

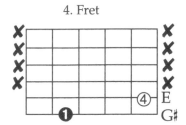

F3

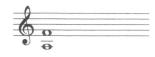

5. Fret

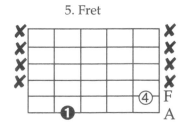

F#3

6. Fret

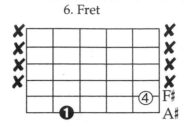

G3

7. Fret

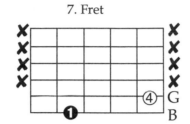

Ab3

8. Fret

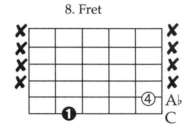

A3

9. Fret

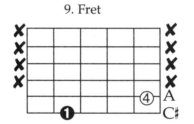

Bb3

10. Fret

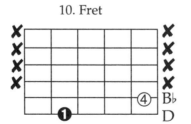

B3

11. Fret

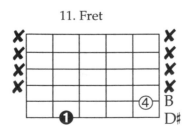

F3

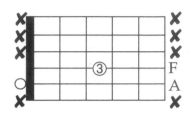

F#3

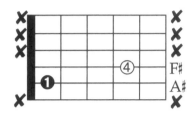

G3

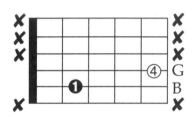

Ab3

3. Fret

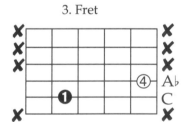

A3

4. Fret

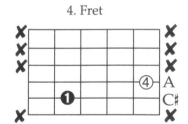

Bb3

5. Fret

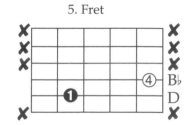

POWER CHORDS

B3

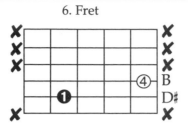

6. Fret

C3

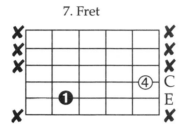

7. Fret

C#3

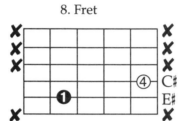

8. Fret

D3

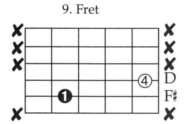

9. Fret

Eb3

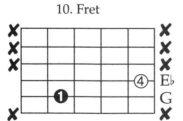

10. Fret

POWER
CHORDS

E3

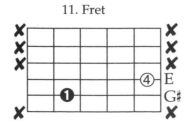

11. Fret

B♭3

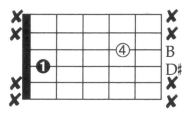

B3

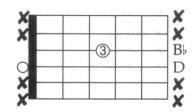

C3

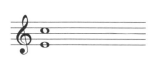
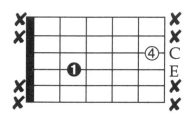

C♯3

3. Fret

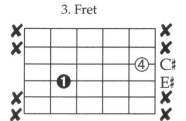

D3

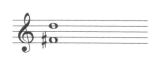

4. Fret

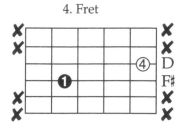

E♭3

5. Fret

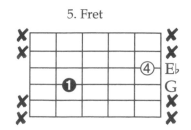

E3

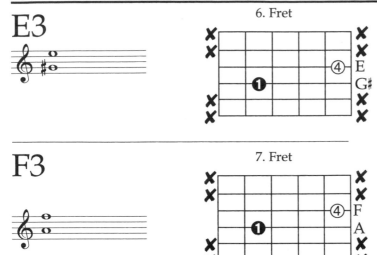

6. Fret

E
G#

F3

7. Fret

F
A

F#3

8. Fret

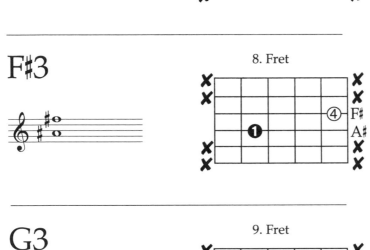

F#
A#

G3

9. Fret

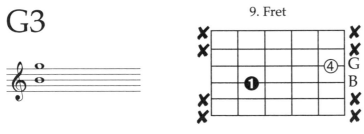

G
B

Ab3

10. Fret

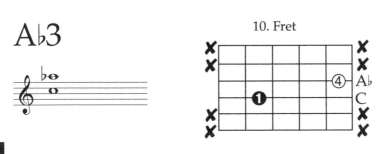

Ab
C

A3

11. Fret

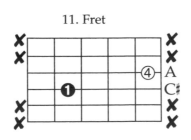

A
C#

E6

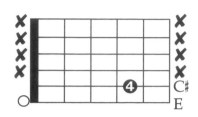

C#
E

F6

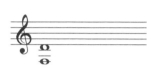

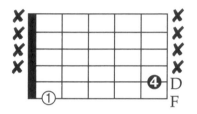

D
F

F#6

2. Fret

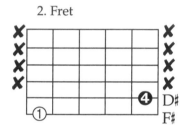

D#
F#

G6

3. Fret

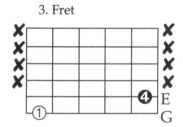

E
G

Ab6

4. Fret

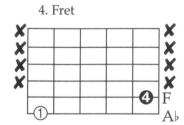

F
Ab

A6

5. Fret

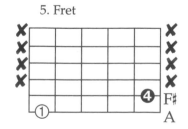

F#
A

B♭6

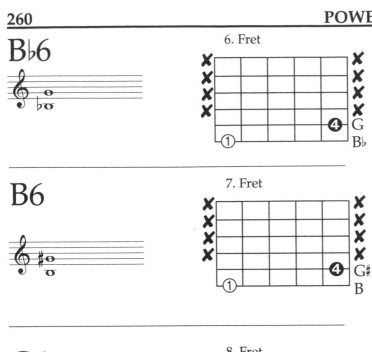

6. Fret

B6

7. Fret

C6

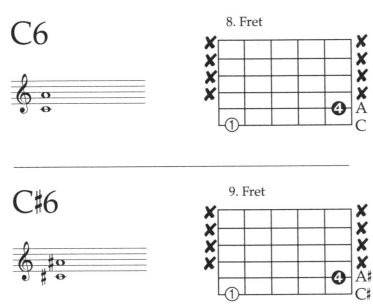

8. Fret

C♯6

9. Fret

D6

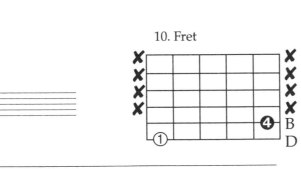

10. Fret

E♭6

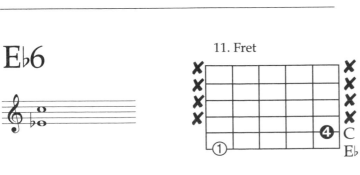

11. Fret

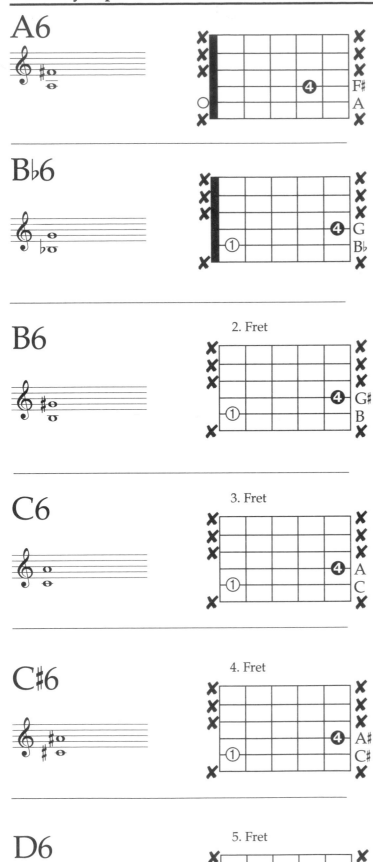

A6

Bb6

B6
2. Fret

C6
3. Fret

C#6
4. Fret

D6
5. Fret

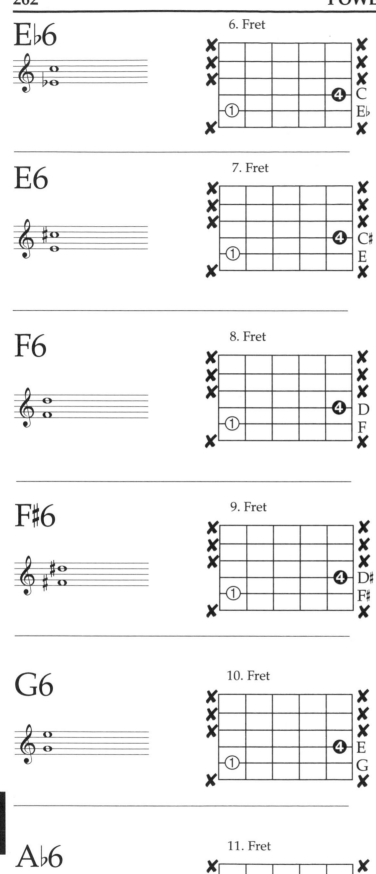

E♭6

6. Fret

E6

7. Fret

F6

8. Fret

F♯6

9. Fret

G6

10. Fret

A♭6

11. Fret

D6

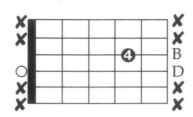

Eb6

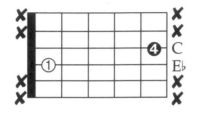

E6

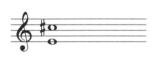

2. Fret

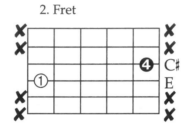

F6

3. Fret

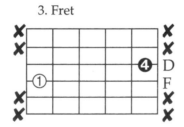

F#6

4. Fret

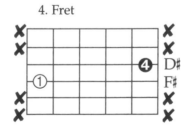

G6

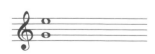

5. Fret

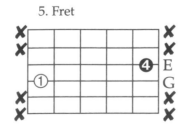

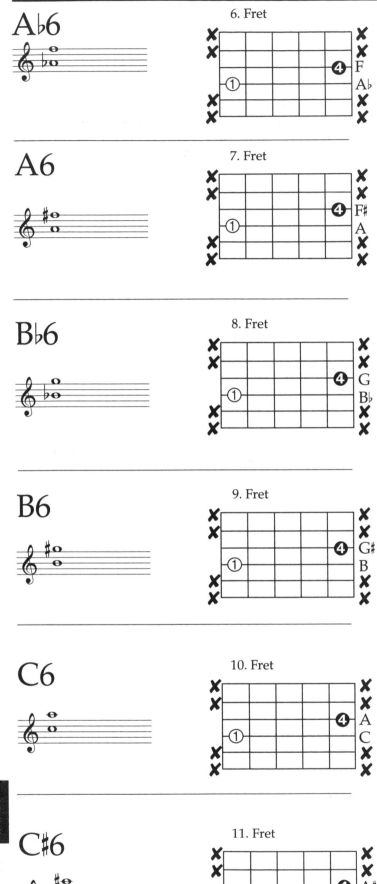

Ab6 — 6. Fret — F, Ab

A6 — 7. Fret — F#, A

Bb6 — 8. Fret — G, Bb

B6 — 9. Fret — G#, B

C6 — 10. Fret — A, C

C#6 — 11. Fret — A#, C#

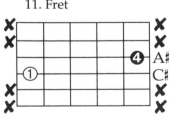

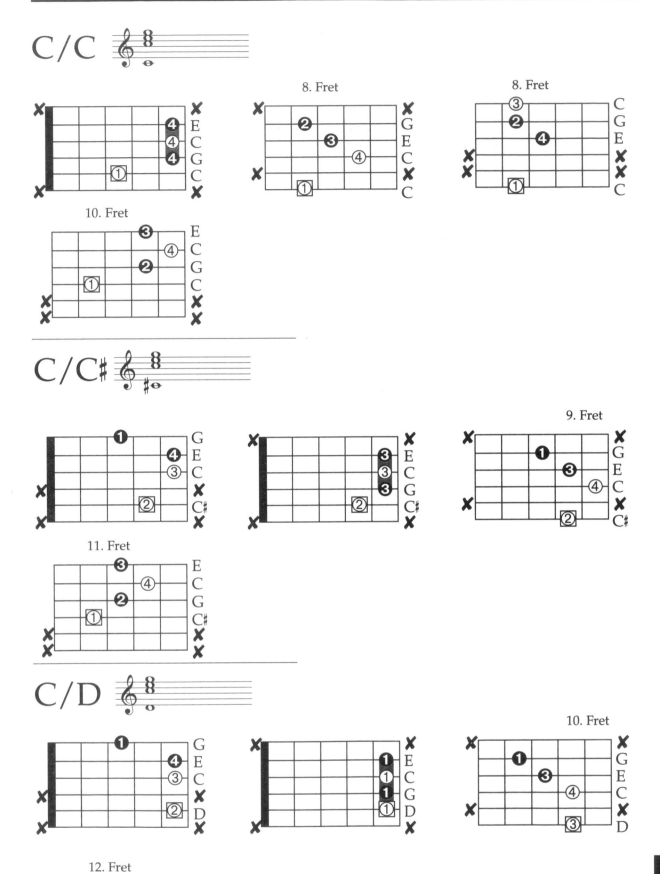

C/E♭

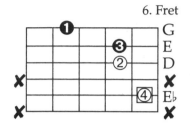 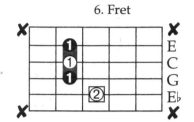 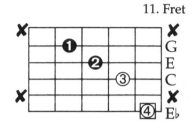

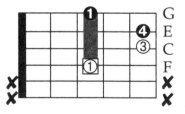

C/E

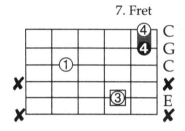 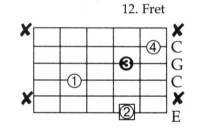 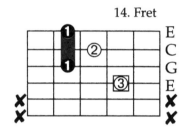

C/F

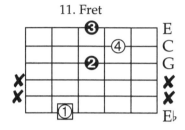 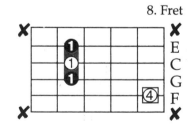 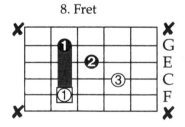

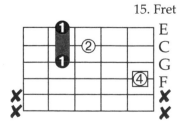

SLASH CHORDS

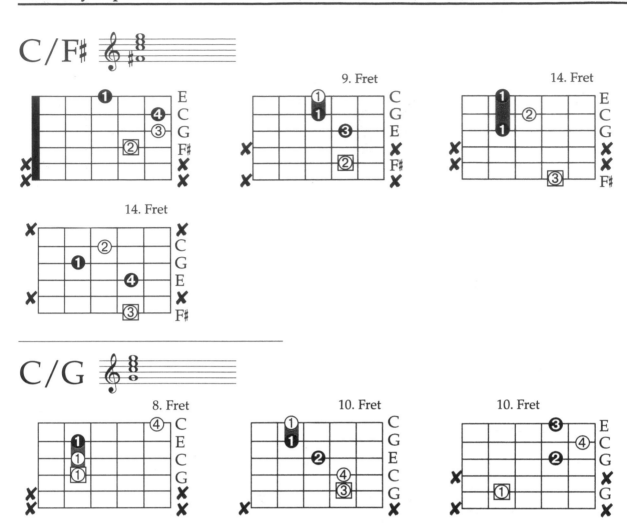

C/F♯

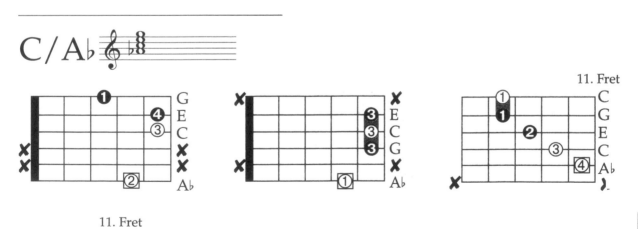

C/G

C/A♭

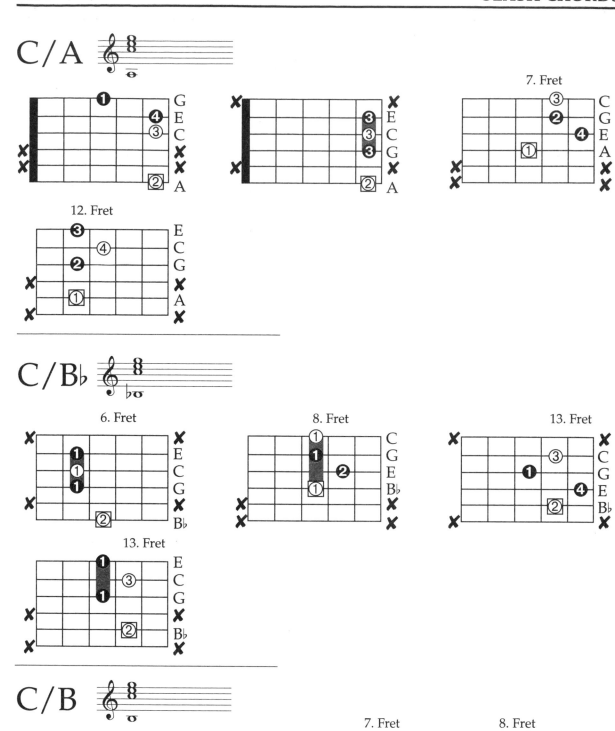

C/A

C/B♭

C/B

Transposing

Transposing is the process of rewriting a melody, chord or piece of music into a different key. The relative note intervals remain the same. Unlike the piano, where transposing a chord to a different key results in different finger positions, the guitarist keeps the same finger positions and merely moves up or down the fretboard. As an example, we'll take a look at the F major bar chord. As you can see, to transpose this chord to F♯ major it is simply a matter of moving up a half-step, or one fret position. To further transpose to a G major chord, the F♯ major chord is moved up one fret position.

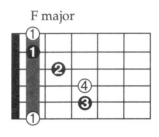
F major

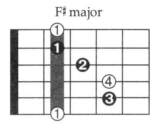
F♯ major

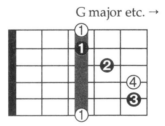
G major etc. →

Not all the possible chords on the guitar reflect this simple relationship - this is particularly not true for chords in the first five frets of the instrument where it becomes necessary to alter the fingering. However, as you become more familiar with this book, you will notice that the majority of chords can be transposed in this manner.